THE MACMILLAN COMPANY
NEW YORK · BOSTON · CHICAGO · DALLAS
ATLANTA · SAN FRANCISCO

MACMILLAN & CO., LIMITED
LONDON · BOMBAY · CALCUTTA
MELBOURNE

THE MACMILLAN COMPANY
OF CANADA, LIMITED
TORONTO

PERENNIALS O

PERENNIALS OF FLOWERLAND

by

ALICE T. A. QUACKENBUSH

Author of "The Annals of Flowerland," etc.

NEW YORK

THE MACMILLAN COMPANY

1929

Set up and printed.
Published October, 1929.

Printed in the United States of America by
J. J. LITTLE AND IVES COMPANY, NEW YORK

INTRODUCTION

The royal road to happiness passes through the garden, in fact, may begin and end there. For to garden successfully is achievement of the finest. Its sturdy requirement can lure youth from less admirable pursuit; its benign serenity makes point to age that usefulness increases with the passing years. Call it tonic, sport, science, art, if you will. But do not fail to call it, adventure.

A certain few will think alone of the beauty of a season and content themselves with sowing seeds of those friends necessary to all who delight in Flowerland, the annuals. Darlings of a year, these are, which ask little and give generous return in gay bloom. Yet a garden made wholly of such must lack something of perfection. For stability and the interest of development through growth are not among their virtues. These more sterling qualities belong to perennials, those bits of green magic which may sleep through Sir Winter's storms to waken in the sweetness of spring. It is good to remember that many are identical with those our great-grandmothers made into nosegays. Nor should we forget that, thanks to the patient care of those who have worked among them since, a few are far lovelier.

Here's to perennials then; we pledge in a cup of nectar! And while they are still tucked safely under a blanket of snow, let's gossip a bit about them. They are impervious to criticism and in their case to know all is not so much to forgive all as—a teasing impossibility.

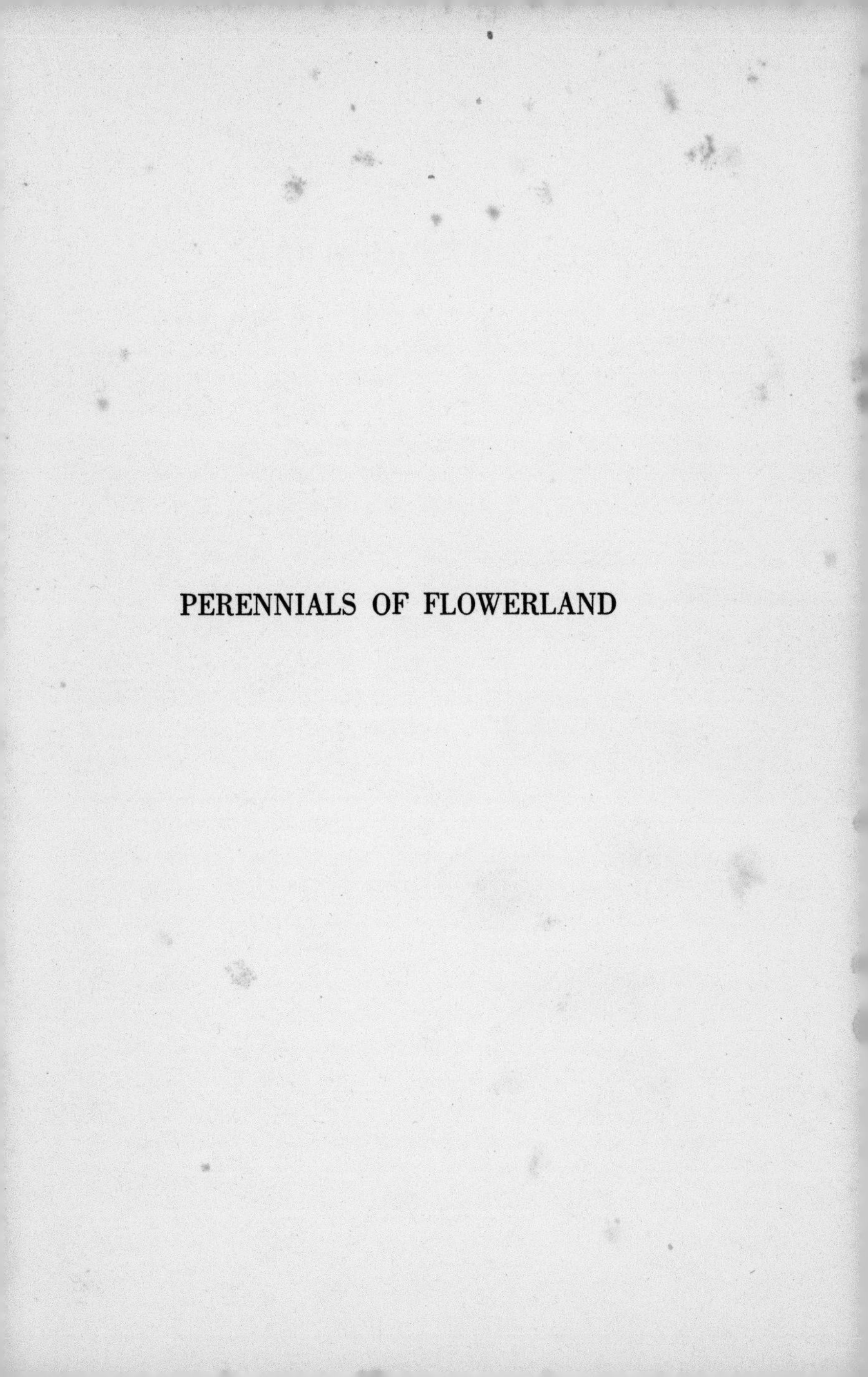

PERENNIALS OF FLOWERLAND

THE ACANTHACEÆ

A large family related to the Scrophulariaceæ. The leaves are opposite and ornamental; in fact it is for their sake that we admit members of the family to the border. The flowers are irregular and not especially ornamental.

ACANTHUS

ACANTHUS

Stately, is the adjective which comes to mind as descriptive of this plant, valuable because of its decorative foliage.

The species, latifolius, has broad, deeply cut leaves and grows, according to the richness of the soil, from three to five feet in height. The flowers are a purplish rose and scarcely a garden necessity.

A. mollis has white or lilac flowers and is slightly shorter than latifolius. Both are natives of the Mediterranean coast and not always hardy farther north. On the other hand, they take kindly to lifting and potting and make good house-plants provided they have plenty of sunshine. In the garden, they should be given a warm, sheltered place, rich soil and an abundance of water. They may be increased by seed or root division.

The name means a spine because some sorts are prickly. A. mollis will probably be remembered when plants of more worthy bloom are forgotten because its leaves inspired the design of the Corinthian capital in Greek architecture. Yet few of us know just how this happened. There is a story to the effect that a little girl died and was buried near an Acanthus. Her nurse placed a basket filled with toys the child had owned near the grave. She set it directly over the plant and its leaves curled gracefully around this love-offering. The sculptor, Callimachus, chanced to see this and perpetuated it in stone.

THE APOCYNACEÆ

The Dogbane Family, which is closely related to the Milkweed (Asclepiadaceæ), is largely tropical. It has a milky juice, sometimes very poisonous, and is valuable, commercially, giving India-rubber, woods for carving and furniture, barks for medicine, and a few edible fruits. Also, such nice annuals as Vinca (Periwinkle) and subjects for the greenhouse such as the Oleander and Cape Jasmine.

The individual flowers are small but clustered in such a way as to be striking. The plants are graceful with leaves of clear green which remain good throughout the season.

AMSONIA

AMSONIA

A. tabernæmontana, sometimes called, latifolia, has charming blooms of light blue which grow in loose panicles and flowers during May, a time when this shade is not plentiful in the garden. It is slow to establish but, once developed, may be divided. A longer method of increasing is by striking cuttings from the tips of non-flowering shoots. The foliage is sightly throughout the summer. Rich loam and a cool place, slightly shaded, suits it best. It grows about two feet high. A native of North America and named for Charles Amson.

THE ARISTOLOCHIACEÆ

Twining vines and low growing plants with curiously shaped, apetalous blooms characterize this small family, the Birthwort, which grows throughout the tropical and temperate zones. Most of them possess bitter or acrid roots.

The vine, Dutchman's Pipe, called thus because of the shape of its flowers, is a prominent member. This grows wild in the southern states and may be successfully cultivated in the north.

ASARUM (*Wild Ginger*)

ASARUM

A. canadense, popularly called, Wild Ginger, has small brownish flowers with stems so short as to be almost hidden by the dark green, kidney-shaped leaves. It blooms in the spring and grows from five to seven inches. Ordinary soil and partial shade suit it best although it is not exacting. Increases rapidly and may be divided easily. Perhaps it is better placed in the wild or rock gardens where the leaves will make an excellent carpet throughout the season.

The name comes from a, not and saron, feminine. The application is not quite clear although it has been suggested that its use as a medicine is too violent save for the strongest.

THE ASCLEPIADACEÆ

The Milkweed Family is beautiful even in its most weedy form, A. cornuti, the common Milkweed of the meadows, with its sweet umbels of greenish lavender bloom and its fruit-pods which delight child and adult alike. Mostly tropical, with many shrubs whose juice is occasionally possessed with emetic or purgative quality. It gives the greenhouse the handsome Carrion-flower and Wax-plant; medicine, a tonic from Indian Sarsaparilla; commerce, Marsdenia, a blue dye resembling indigo.

ASCLEPIAS

ASCLEPIAS

From a plant bearing the Greek name for the physician, Æsculapius, we expect much—and are not disappointed. A. tuberosa, better known as Butterfly Weed because it attracts these dainty creatures, is a lovely thing. In rich soil and full sunshine it grows three feet in height and by midsummer bears umbels of waxy flowers, bright orange in color. For finest effect, it should be placed near blue. Stokesia and Platycodon are blooming at this time, also the second flowering of Centaurea montana, to mention perennials, while the annuals Centaurea cyanus, if not allowed to seed, and blue Asters, if sown under glass, will serve as especially lovely supplements.

Although this is a native of North America, it does not always ripen seeds in northern gardens; however it may be divided in the spring.

THE BIGNONIACEÆ

Tropical for the most part and especially abundant in South America. The family consists largely of trees and shrubby climbers. The trees usually have hard, close-grained wood—calabash pipes are made from that of the Crescentia.

The Catalpa is the chief tree representative of the temperate zone and the Trumpet-creeper (Bignonia), the best known vine.

INCARVILLEA

INCARVILLEA

Decorative either in the border or the greenhouse. Variety I. Dalavayi has Begonia-shaped blooms of rose with yellow throats. It grows about two feet high with deeply cut leaves and flowers from June to September.

Sandy soil with leaf mold is its preference. Seeds should be sown indoors or in the coldframe and as early as possible. Plants may be divided in the fall but this must be done carefully. The roots are fleshy and all growth of this character does not take kindly to being disturbed. Named for Incarville, a botanical correspondent of the French botanist, Jussieu.

THE BORAGINACEÆ

Blue is the gift of the Borages to Flowerland. To be sure, some species have varieties of other color, yet the first choice is invariably from the blues—for certainly no one would be so ungrateful as to think of the family which includes the unforgettable Forget-me-not without doing honor to this color.

It comprises shrubs, herbs, annuals, perennials; a large and altogether lovely gathering.

ANCHUSA

MERTENSIA

MYOSOTIS (*Forget-me-not*)

ANCHUSA

The perennial Anchusas of garden worth all come from species A. italica, a native of the Mediterranean. Probably all lovers of this plant know that it owes a great part of its present beauty to workers at the Dropmore estate in England; so much in fact that A. italica, variety Dropmore is grown almost exclusively. This is from three to four feet high and in June bears quantities of deep blue blooms which look like huge Forget-me-nots. The period of bloom is all too short and as the plant is rather unsightly afterwards, it should be placed at the back of the border. A named variety, the Opal, has slightly shorter plants, slightly smaller blooms, but these are lighter in color, the true Forget-me-not shade.

Give a rich soil and a warm sunny situation. If drainage is not perfect or the season wet, the fleshy roots will often rot. On this account, it is well to sow a few seeds each year. It is also possible to increase by root-cuttings in the fall, a method which although more difficult, has the merit of insuring the exact color of the parent plant.

The name means a cosmetic because one species was formerly used as a skin dye.

MERTENSIA

This lovely thing of spring has light blue blooms and follows the good example of its relative, Forget-me-not, in wearing pink in budhood. It flowers in loose panicles, has deep green leaves and grows about two feet high. M. virginica, the Virginian Cowslip, is the species universally grown. Unless given partial shade, its life will be short. Ordinary soil is acceptable and good drainage necessary. There is one bad habit which should always be borne in mind; the leaves wither quickly after bloom has passed, leaving no indication of the beauty which has been. Remember this when you plant and, what is more important, recall it when you cultivate. At least once each season I am reduced to panic for fear that I have thoughtlessly wrought destruction to loveliness.

It may be raised from seed but root division, either in spring or autumn, is a shorter, better method. Named for a German botanist, Mertens.

MYOSOTIS

Mouse's ear is the translation of this word, the scientific name for Forget-me-not and given because of the shape of the leaves.

Is it too much to say that a garden is not a garden at all without this gentle, low-growing creature? It is amenable to any soil; prefers partial shade yet will do without it; self-seeds readily. Its only insistence is an abundance of water and what the sky occasionally refuses, the watering-can should supply in gratitude for loveliness. The perennial sorts flower heavily in the spring and a second blooming in the fall is not unusual. Still if one desires bloom throughout the season—and who does not?—annuals must fill in during midsummer.

Tales from many lands cluster about the plant as closely as the florets around its stem. Although I have cited a few (note—The Annuals of Flowerland, page 9), here is one which simply must be told. An old, old story from Persia and of an angel who was so indiscreet as to love a mortal thereby forfeiting his place in paradise. To be sure he had first seen the fair one while dressing her hair with these blue blossoms. If this were golden, who shall blame him? Yet he was forbidden by the keeper of the pearly gate to reënter till the maiden should scatter seed of the flower which had contributed to his undoing over the face of the globe.

They wandered for years, these two, till at last, the

task completed, they stood before the judge with the flaming sword. It is good to find that because of the woman's untiring devotion, both were allowed to pass within.

THE CAMPANULACEÆ

This family, which is mostly herbaceous, lives by choice in the northern temperate zone; a fact which explains its good habit of wintering well in a cold place.

It may be distinguished by a milky juice and bell-shaped flowers with, alas, no fragrance. Blue is the prevailing color, from very dark as in annual Lobelia to true Forget-me-not. Often called the Bellwort Family.

ADENOPHORA
CAMPANULA
JASIONE
LOBELIA
PLATYCODON
PHYTEUMA

ADENOPHORA

Better known by the cottager's name, Bush Ladybell, given because of the shape of the plant as well as that of the flowers; yet not so well known as it merits. The color of all varieties is blue. Perhaps A. potanini is especially to be recommended. This grows about two feet high and prefers rich soil and full sunshine. It does not transplant easily because of the character of the roots and should be increased by seed.

The name, from aden, a gland and phoreo, to bear, was given because of the fleshy disk in the center of each flower.

CAMPANULA

The name is the diminutive of campana and means a little bell; the plant the most prominent of Family Campanulaceæ. All species are useful for the garden and a few necessary if one wishes the Old World touch. Seeds germinate quickly, seedlings require no especial care in transplanting, ordinary soil suffices, stock may be increased by root division: in fact no coddling is needed at any time during a plant's life span with the slight exception that staking for the taller sorts in a windy location is a wise precaution.

The following varieties are the best known:

C. carpatica (Carpathian Harebell), a charming edging with good foliage throughout the season and a mass of blue bell-like blooms in June (variety alba is white of course). If one has leisure plus patience to cut the blossoms the flowering season will be slightly prolonged. This is a task! It sometimes self-seeds yet if one needs new plants it is scarcely safe to depend on this. Root division is simple and invariably successful.

C. medium (Canterbury Bells)—best known, best loved of them all; given this popular name because of their shape which is like those others the pilgrims bound for Canterbury were wont to carry. Unfortunately they are biennials yet worth the extra care the name implies. They should be started outside the garden and transplanted the first fall or second spring. Cut the withered blooms and others will appear on the same stalk. The double varieties are popular yet the singles, at least to my way of thinking, are more graceful. Flower stalks are about two feet high and blooms white, pink or blue.

C. persicæfolia (peach-leaved Bell-flower), very like Canterbury Bell in flower but differing in leaf, as the specific name indicates, and a true perennial.

C. pyramidalis, popularly called the chimney Bell-flower because of its height. The blooms are smaller than those of the preceding two species and either Forget-me-not blue or white. Although a perennial it is rather tender and should be carefully protected. Because of this quality it is usually grown in the greenhouse.

C. rotundifolia, a wee thing, six to twelve inches high and growing in compact clumps. It is famous as the Blue Bell of Scotland. Perhaps the rockery is the best home for it. Unlike most of its relatives it will flourish in partial shade.

JASIONE

A far too little known rock plant with blue flowers tipped by fuzz, growing in heads somewhat like the Armerias and appearing midsummer. Like many of the less usual Alpines, it asks special soil condition—in this case sand enriched by a little peat. Also, it is well to give winter protection. Increase by seed.

LOBELIA

The gorgeous Cardinal Flower (Lobelia cardinalis) which is at its best flaming near the water's edge, may be enticed into the garden if one bear in mind its partiality to wet feet and shade. It is a native of the United States and should be cherished as one of her valuable possessions. Never deplete the countryside by removing it. Where it grows wild, you may be sure that it not only is happy but may bring happiness to the passer-by. If you wish it for your own garden, buy from a nurseryman who propagates in quantity.

It blooms in August and is so scarlet a tone as to require careful placing. Once established it may be divided in the spring but not in the fall. Perhaps the safer way is to raise from seed. Give winter protection; in a cold climate it may be dug and the roots stored the same as those of the Dahlia.

The Lobelias were named for the botanist Lobel who was a physician to James I.

PLATYCODON

Mix a bit of sand with your ordinary garden soil, be sure of good drainage, set roots of the Platycodon, and by midsummer you will have not alone the bell-like flowers which characterize this family but before them, interesting balloon-shaped buds which are responsible for the name, Japanese Balloon Flower.

The plants grow about two feet high and the blooms are either white or dark blue, also mauve, although this is dullish and rather uninteresting. They do not divide easily; it is better to increase stock by seeds or cuttings. The stalks are somewhat weak and the plant better in appearance when staked. If you wish to cut for the house be sure to do this before the sun is high.

The name comes from platys, broad, and hodon, bell, because of the shape of the blossom.

PHYTEUMA

There are many Phyteumas, often called Rampions, although few are listed by American seedsmen. This is probably because our climate, at least in the north, does not suit them. One species, P. scheuchzeri, may be grown successfully in a warm spot of either border or rockery. It grows about a foot high and bears fuzzy, blue flower-heads in June. Sandy loam enriched by leaf-mold pleases it best.

THE CARYOPHYLLACEÆ

Do you realize that the vegetable bane known as Chickweed and the garden delight, the Pink, are relatives? It must be occasion for boasting to Chickweed. But how about Pink? Probably she is too fine a lady to care over-much.

The Caryophyllaceæ or Pink Family to which both belong, is a large one distributed throughout the globe. It is uneven as to merit. There are many other weeds, also charming garden flowers. All may be recognized by a slight swelling at the nodes.

Perhaps the supreme gift of the Pink, its most distinguished member, is a haunting fragrance.

ALSINE
ARENARIA
CERASTIUM (*Snow-in-Summer*)
DIANTHUS (*Pink or Carnation*)
GYPSOPHILA (*Angel's or Infant's Breath*)
LYCHNIS
SAPONARIA
SILENE (*Catchfly*)
TUNICA

ALSINE

Although obviously a relative of Chickweed and sometimes called by that name of unpleasant memory, her nice tufts of foliage should give little Alsine a place in the rockery wherever something not exacting as to soil is required. It is a convenient plant for use when a rock-garden is young and its owner new to the lore of soil requirements for more difficult subjects. The flowers are white and the name one which carries planting directions. It is from alsos, a grove, which certainly should warn the keeper of the garden that partial shade is a necessity.

ARENARIA

Another wee, white-flowered resident of the rockery, sometimes called Moss Sandwort. Its name, from arena, sand, speaks for itself. The plant makes dense mats of bright green foliage which creeps over and seems to cling to the rocks and stones nearby. Blooms appear during June and July. Division is more simple than increasing by seed; these should be shaded and kept moist till well rooted.

CERASTIUM

An excellent edging because of its silvery gray foliage and also popular in the rock-garden. If used as an edging it should be cut back after the mass of white flowers have passed; otherwise it becomes sprawly and the center browns. Ordinary soil is satisfactory and it may be increased by seed, division or cuttings from the bloomless shoots. The name means a horn and was given because of the shape of the seed-pods. It is sometimes libeled by the name Mouse-eared Chickweed.

DIANTHUS

One of the queens of perfume; named from dios, divine and anthos, a flower, the divine flower it is, and surely he who gave the name was rarely discriminating. They are usually called Pinks because of the prevailing color and may be known by gray foliage and the prominent nodes of the stems. All add grace and much fragrance to their abiding place.

D. Allwoodi is a strong strain of plants with fragrant flowers several to a stalk which have a long period of bloom. There are named varieties such as Harold, a double white; Jean, white with a violet center; Mary, light rose with a maroon center; Robert, deep rose, maroon center. They are desirable because of their permanence and good for the border's foreground.

D. barbatus (Sweet William). The name Sweet William carries us back to old gardens and I confess to a weakness for those quaint, mottled blooms reminiscent of the vogue for calico. I am in minority for this and willingly concede that hybridizers have wrought marvels in fixing color; you may have pure white, pinks in variety, scarlets and maroon. Seedlings, and Sweet William is a prodigal self-sower, do not always come true; bees, you know, care not at all for gardening color schemes.

It is a biennial yet once in the garden, will always remain there if allowed to self-seed, which after all is the pleasantest way of getting new plants if one is not too exacting as to color.

D. cæsius (Chedder or Cliff Pink), a tiny plant with light rose, fragrant blooms; delightful as an edging. The flowering period is early and short yet because of the scent which is of that old-fashioned, musky sort, it is too precious to lose.

D. deltoides (Maiden Pink), especially suited to the rockery. It seldom reaches more than six inches in height and is not so fragrant as D. cæsius. On the other hand and as partial compensation, it may be either white, pink or bright red.

D. plumarius (Pheasant's Eye Pink). Its popular name comes from the shape of the center marking. This is the hardiest species and a fine edging. In June the fringed blossoms are lifted on strong stems a foot above the gray foliage and, if cut, will continue to flower slightly throughout the summer. Unfortunately it is not so sweet-scented as one might wish. There are both singles and doubles, the double sometimes have the bad habit of breaking at the calyx.

Pinks are sun-lovers and grow most successfully in light soil. They are easily increased by division, cuttings, pegging or seeds.

A flower of such beauty of form and color which carries in addition the unseen charm of fragrance; one sufficiently catholic as to be dedicated to both Venus and the Virgin, as would be expected has gathered to itself the interest of legend. I have mentioned this before. (Note—"The Annuals Of Flowerland," p. 21.)

GYPSOPHILA

The botanical name of this enchanting gift to the garden means chalk-loving while the popular, more often used, Infant's Breath, is not alone descriptive but serves as an indication of the high regard in which the plant is held by the human race. "We need's must love——"

At the spring awakening, it throws shoots from two to three feet high and these bear gray, rather insignificant leaves followed in midsummer by numberless blooms of grayish white so tiny as to seem like a gracious overtone. A gentle presence this which can do no wrong either in garden or bouquet.

G. paniculata, a single, is the more romantic; G. flore pleno to be sure, may be handsomer yet like many another, it seems to have sacrificed some of the birthright to ethereal loveliness for the mode. G. repens, a wee trailer with white or rose blooms, should not be forgotten. It is worthy a place in the rockery.

Roots are fleshy and do not take kindly to transplanting, in fact if they are disturbed at all, it is better to make root cuttings although one must lose the original plant. For peace of mind, the safer method is to make cuttings from shoots directly after bloom has passed. It must be acknowledged that plants grown from seed are sturdier than all others though one must wait longer for blooming time.

LYCHNIS

A study in contrasts, Gypsophila and Lychnis; for where the first is soft and amenable to any companionship, the other is a hard, flaming personality named because of this fact from luchnos, a lamp. It should be placed carefully, either among soft blues or with such neutrals as its Gypsophila relatives. Gay and abundant bloom give it value.

Like the less flamboyant Infant's Breath, it is best increased by seed although that of the doubles does not always mature. These may be divided in the early autumn—because of the different formation, root-division is more simple than with Gypsophila. Rich soil seems consistent with such high colorings.

There are several species, beginning with L. alpina—to speak in terms of alphabet. This, as the name suggests is an Alpine: it grows from five to six inches high and, in May, bears compact little heads of pink bloom delightful for the rockery. L. chalcedonica, the Maltese or Jerusalem Cross, is from two to three feet high and has scarlet flowers larger than usual to the genus and borne in umbels. My favorite, because of its association with old-world gardening, is L. coronaria, Mullein Pink.

A frank magenta, notwithstanding its cool gray leaves, it must be given intelligent placing. After the flowering stalks have served their purpose, cut them off and the leaf rosettes at the base will ornament the garden till frost. It self-seeds almost too freely when one remembers the more than likely mis-association of such vivid tone.

The Haageana hybrids give greater variety in color; pink, salmons, scarlet of course, and white—though I for one see no need for a white Lychnis. If you want to be sure of any special shade in new plants, it is well to take root-cuttings.

SAPONARIA

S. vaccaria, the best known and perhaps most satisfactory, is an annual, nice for both garden and house as a blender. S. ocymoides, a low trailer with trusses of scarlet bloom, is perennial. It flowers in midsummer and is most effective creeping over rocks. Easily increased by cuttings.

The name comes from soap because the bruised leaves make a lather. This is especially noticeable in good old Bouncing Bet (S. officinalis) of the fields.

SILENE

The Silenes are named from sialon, saliva, because the leaves bear a sticky substance which is so fatal in entangling small insects as to merit the descriptive word, Catchfly. Most of them are classed as weeds rather than flowers. Three of the perennials are worthy garden-room. S. alpestris, six inches high with glossy green leaves and white blooms; S. Schafta, about the same size with rose-colored flowers; S. Fortunei, from one to two feet high with pink, slightly fringed blooms.

Ordinary soil is satisfactory. Increase by seed or cuttings of the non-flowering shoots.

TUNICA

A small, but charming, rock plant with tiny pink flowers in midsummer. Give it rich soil and increase by seed or divisions in spring.

The name is the Latin form for a tunic or coat.

THE CISTACEÆ

A lowly family, at least in manner of growth; even the shrubs are dwarf. The leaves are usually of a deep green and the blooms, although showy, ephemeral. Rock rose is a popular name given to several members. For the most part, natives of the Mediterranean coast.

HELIANTHEMUM (*Rock-rose*)

HELIANTHEMUM

Give any plant which is named for helios, the sun, plenty of it. In case of this one, sand in the soil will also benefit assuring plenty of heat.

A trailer in habit with evergreen foliage, it is commonly called Rock rose. H. mutabile is the most interesting. During July and August many blooms appear which are unusual in that they are often a soft pink at opening, changing to lavender and, before fading, to almost white. Occasionally they are yellow.

Increase by seed or cuttings—cuttings of course when the shade is especially good.

THE COMMELINACEÆ

A family which delights in heat. It is almost entirely herbaceous and low of growth. It may be recognized by the three green sepals and three or even two petals of the flower. The foliage is glossy and decorative throughout the season. There seem to be no members which are used either as herbs or medicine.

TRADESCANTIA (*Flower-of-a-Day*)

TRADESCANTIA

Although a native of the United States, this useful plant is named for a gardener of the household of James I—this because it was first given to certain tropical varieties grown by him.

T. virginica will grow anywhere but is especially nice near water because of the iris-like quality of the foliage. It is a rank grower and soon forms clumps of leaves notable for conspicuous purple veining. The flowers are deep blue and borne in terminal umbels. It is called Flower-of-the-Day because the life of an individual bloom is no longer than this period. In common with other members of the Commelinaceæ Family, it is often known as Spiderwort.

T. vulgaris, a creeper with broader leaves, is the blue, three-petaled wildling of the fields. Both are sufficiently hardy to divide in full bloom.

THE COMPOSITÆ

The Composites were so named by early botanists because of a mistaken belief that their blooms are compound. This is not a fact; what appears to be a single flower, in reality, is a group of many surrounded by a collar of brightly colored bracts.

This is the largest family in plant life and grows wherever vegetation is to be found. There are a few shrubs and herbs to its credit, also such edibles as artichoke, salsify and lettuce; even an occasional member with medicinal property. But its showy flowering plants make it especially notable for ornament. A generous family this! For up to the time of killing frost, when all other blooms have fallen by the wayside, certain members will still be going strong—in fact, may be considered Nature's kindest gift to the fall garden. Fragrance, unfortunately, is usually lacking; still such gallant bloom and gay color are welcome necessities.

ACHILLEA
ANTHEMIS
ARTEMISIA (*Wormwood*)
ASTER (*Michaelmas Daisy*)
BELLIS (*English Daisy*)
BOLTONIA
BUPHTHALMUM
CATANANCHE

CENTAUREA
CHRYSANTHEMUM
COREOPSIS
DORONICUM
ECHINACEA
ECHINOPS
ERIGERON
EUPATORIUM
GAILLARDIA (*Blanket Flower*)
HELENIUM
HELIANTHUS (*Sunflower*)
HELIOPSIS
INULA
LEONTOPODIUM (*Edelweiss*)
LIATRIS
PYRETHRUM
STOKESIA
TANACETUM

ACHILLEA

In common with most Composites, the Achillea is quite content with ordinary soil. It prefers sunshine, yet will grow in partial shade, increases easily; is in fact, a garden subject asking little care. Whatever attention you give will be along the line of keeping it from becoming so large as to encroach on more delicate growth. This is understandable when one remembers that the common Yarrow of the roadside is a near relative.

It was named for Achilles because his tutor, Chiron, used it as a medicine.

There are several good species, among them, A. ageratum, an Alpine which from the name one might hope to find blue; it is yellow and slightly scented.

A. ptarmica (the Pearl) is the finest. It grows about two feet high and beginning in June, bears a wealth of tiny balls of pure white. If the flower stalks are cut it makes quick recovery and will bloom slightly till frost. The foliage is always good and it is excellent for cutting. Variety Perry's White has larger blooms than the older form.

A. millefolium var. roseum is a crimson variety of the common Yarrow. I do not care greatly for it, although it has the virtue of late bloom. A. tomentosa, a six inch Alpine with yellow flowers will flourish in a spot too dry for most growth.

ANTHEMIS

Although not alone in bearing flowers profusely, Anthemis, because of it, is called for the word meaning flower. It has in addition a rugged constitution and will succeed with little moisture and in any soil. A. tintoria, called Camomile, grows about a foot high and has daisy-like blooms of golden yellow. It is easily increased by seed or division as is the handsomer A. Kelwayi (Hardy Marguerite) which may be had in various shades of yellow.

ARTEMISIA

Useful for fall flowering, the Artemisia, which grows at least four feet high and up to blooming time gives the impression of a sturdy shrub for all its finely cut leaves. When the creamy white, sweetly scented flowers appear, it is as if the garden is graced by a late-blooming Spiræa. Nice for flower arrangements. Ordinary soil and a dry location, for growing condition; root division in spring or cuttings, for increase.

Named for Artemis, the Greek Diana. Such unequal offerings to humanity as Tarregon and Wormwood, aptly called Herb of Forgetfulness because Absinthe is made from it, are to be found among the more utilitarian species.

ASTER

Why grow perennial Asters when one may have their lovelier annual relatives? To begin, with the exception of similarity of blossom form, they are vastly different. The perennials, called Michaelmas Daisies because they are at the height of flower on Michaelmas Day, grow to tall shrubby plants which make excellent background for earlier bloom—and when they do flower, are generosity itself. They will grow in any soil; are amenable to either drought or drench; will survive a bit of frost; and are *not* attractive to beetles. Why grow them? Why not!

As matter of fact, although the gardeners of England have long appreciated their loveliness, with us, perennial Asters are just coming into their own. And now that they are finding adequate place in our plantings and our hearts, we learn that there are far more species than former indifference deserves. One may have pinks, blues, mauves, even white if you will, and in named varieties too numerous to catalogue.

They divide readily and are the better for it. The name, which means a star, seems perfect.

BELLIS

"Wee, modest, crimson-tippèd flower," sang Robert Burns, of Bellis, the little English Daisy of the fields. We have welcomed it to the garden, this breath of innocence, which is well. We have gone further and developed a so-called Giant Strain, which is ill—decidedly. Perfection is perfection, you know. When in addition we have the temerity to change its white to pink, the hapless wildling loses its all of charm and modesty. Instead of a "modest, crimson-tippèd" delight it becomes just another pink bloom. Bobbie of Scotland would have liked the metamorphosis as little as some folk will what I have said.

Just remember that Bellis was once a dryad and has already been changed once, into a flower that the god of fruit trees might always keep her near him. Let the poor girl alone!

BOLTONIA

Perhaps "useful" is the word which best expresses Boltonia. It may be tucked in anywhere at the back of the border, where its trim leaves will pass almost unnoticed till on some day of early fall you will find the plant a mass of pinkish-white buds. Some morning soon after, when you step into the garden, you will think it covered by snow, so closely set and so glisteny white are its flowers. Nice, vegetable snow this which melts away all too soon.

If soil be rich, the white, universally grown species, B. asteroides, will reach a height of eight feet. Although a bit shorter in consequence, it is perfectly happy in ordinary soil. For planting among early-flowering shrubs it is unsurpassed.

A newer species, B. latisquama, is shorter and with blooms of lavender-pink. Both are good for cutting, increase easily by division and will withstand a slight frost. Native of America and named for the botanist, Bolton.

BUPHTHALMUM

A rather appalling name which means ox's eye and given because of the large eye-like disc in the center of the flowerheads. Ox-eye, as it is popularly called, seems nicer, yet for identification, Buphthalmum it must be—there are other ox-eyes in Flowerland.

B. salicifolium is about two feet high and flowers in September. It likes ordinary soil and, in common with most bearers of sturdy yellow blooms, full sunlight. Root-division is simple; so much so that it seems unnecessary labor to bother with seed.

CATANANCHE

The Greek word, hatanangke, means a strong incentive, and a nice, popular name for the plant, Cupid's Dart, gives understanding of the particular incentive for which it was famed in the classic world. To be sure the daisy-like blooms—C. cœrulea, when light blue; C. alba, when white, do not look like anybody's dart. It's the potency of the plant itself which merits such. There is a story that it was used in love potions when these were reputed more efficacious than our less credulous age admits.

However it still keeps charm for the garden, the narrow, gray-green leaves see to that. It grows two feet high in ordinary soil, may be easily divided or raised each year from seed, possibly the better method for, although a perennial, it shares the love god's distaste for prolonged cold.

CENTAUREA

The annual Centaureas are among the best known flowers of the garden; always included in the tyro's list because of their easy culture and worthy place in that of the most experienced. The perennials are perhaps not so widely known as their relatives, yet they have the same sturdy qualities; ask only ordinary soil, divide easily, seed abundantly.

C. dealbata blooms in midsummer. It grows one to one and a half feet high, has whitish-green foliage and stems, reddish blossoms.

C. macrocephala (large-headed), also flowers in midsummer. The plant is taller, from three to five feet, and the blooms, yellow.

C. montana, called perennial Cornflower or Bachelor Button, is the best known and deservedly. It blooms as early as June and if the plant is cut to the ground directly after will give a second flowering in September. Although there are white and lavender varieties, the original color, cornflower-blue, is far better.

The Centaureas were named, according to a story from Ovid, because the centaur, Chiron, was supposed to have cured a wound by the leaves.

CHRYSANTHEMUM

A gift of China, the Chrysanthemum, which, Englished, means gold flower. It is the glory of the fall garden. In common with other late blooming plants, it should be set in the spring. When division is desirable, and this is often both for the sake of bloom and increase of stock, it should be done as soon as the first stalks appear. Unless one has a greenhouse to carry them through the winter, cuttings must be made before buds appear. Rich, heavy soil gives best result.

Chrysanthemum culture has reached a high mark and, even outdoors, one may have several types and many varieties. Pompoms, Buttons, Anemones or Quills, are adequately descriptive; the Japanese have loose, rather large flowers shaggy in appearance. There are singles and doubles, whites, pinks, scarlets and yellows from the lightest to deep bronze. Species differ somewhat in blooming time and for a northern garden the early are surer of beating a killing frost.

Probably everyone knows that those monster blooms dear to the heart of the florist are the product of greenhouse forcing, heavy feeding and cruel disbudding. They have little in common with the garden varieties where profusion rather than size is desired.

Because of the lasting quality of the bloom, the plants are reputed to give long life. An interesting Chinese legend runs to the effect that Chrysanthemum possesses that Fata Morgana of the ages, the elixir of life. There is record of a certain emperor so cruel of nature as to place longevity in a far from favorable light before his subjects. He heard of this marvel plant and naturally was eager to test its quality, but was told that it lost potency unless picked by one pure of heart. Undoubtedly the old rascal would have preferred to find the treasure by himself; possession as well as knowledge is power, you know. But the condition made that impossible for both him and his court. A young physician suggested a way out of the difficulty. He proposed that a band of three hundred youths and three hundred maidens make the quest. He himself would go along, whether in professional capacity or as chaperon is not told. They journeyed a long distance to the land which is now called Japan. This much is known—and nothing more. Did they find the flower? Did they, perchance, realize that to be out of reach of the tyrant was elixir enough? Who shall say! They never returned.

COREOPSIS

Blooms of guinea-gold, the size of a daisy but with wider petals, which will flower throughout the season with only a moderate amount of cutting. The stems, although slender, are stiff and, as the blossoms keep well, it is ideal for indoors. The leaves of C. lanceolata, the species universally grown, are deeply cleft: include them in your arrangement and by all means add a few buds—wee balls of shiny green which at the same time, withhold and promise.

There are unwise folk who cherish the belief that a plant such as this, which is hardy, flowers heavily, seeds freely, will grow in ordinary soil, is unworthy place in a fine garden. How absurdly wrong! I disagree so completely as to say that wherever blooms of gold some two feet high are suitable, there is nothing so good. When will we learn that the vegetation congenial to climate and condition and not the exotic is Nature's supreme gift?

C. verticillata has smaller flowers which come later than the better known, lanceolata. The only reason for bringing it into the garden is that it is shorter and, of course, there is occasional need for just this.

The name, from koris, bug and opsis, like, seems rather absurd till one looks at the seeds which it must be admitted resemble this garden bane.

DORONICUM

The Doronicum is distinctive for two quite different facts: the lesser important, its derivation from a tongue unusual in plant nomenclature, the Arabic; the other that it is the first member of Family Compositæ to come into flower.

The plant is not grown as frequently as merit deserves —why, I do not know because it is in all respect amenable to reason. Although preferring a rich soil, this is not essential, seed germination is easy, root division, simple. Added to this, the blooms keep well indoors and at the time when there are no others available of similar form. Popularly called Leopard's Bane, it might more accurately be considered, Early Garden's Boon.

D. caucasicum, the only species generally known in the United States, is about two feet high and has marguerite-like blossoms of a clear yellow. Give it a chance and you will never be without it.

ECHINACEA

From echinos, a hedgehog, because of the bristly bracts between the florets.

When it is E. purpurea, it is also purple Cone-flower, growing from three to four feet high, coming to bloom late, sometimes even September, when anything is welcome. A native of North America, often and with justice called, Rudbeckia, because it differs in color alone from that treasure of the meadow, Black-eyed Susan (R. hirta).

Thrives under any condition, although responding gallantly to rich soil and moisture.

ECHINOPS

A plant with name-root similar to that of Echinacea although given for a different reason. Echinacea, you recall, suggests the hedgehog because of the bristles growing between bracts; Echinops, by the addition of a word-root used often in Plantland (opsis, like), describes the bristle-covered flowerheads. Popularly called, Globe Thistle, because of its shape and scratchy appearance.

E. ritro, from two to three feet high, has blooms of deep blue: E. humilis cyanea, grows somewhat higher with blossoms slightly lighter in color. Both flower in midsummer and make excellent dry bouquets for winter. They divide easily and seed almost too freely. Ordinary soil.

ERIGERON

In common parlance known as Fleabane—there are many banes in the family, this surely unneeded to a decent human save in sandy, desert condition where, as matter of fact, it helps not at all, not growing there.

In form, another delightful Daisy, this time with yellow center—an added delight. Place in full sunlight, for although it takes kindly to a bit of moisture, in shade, the plant takes on an ungainly growth.

Hardy. Divide in spring or early fall. Ordinary soil suffices. E. glaucus is a light lavender; E. speciosus, blue, both with the characteristic yellow center.

The name, er, spring and geron, an old man, is given because of a downy fuzz on the leaves when they first appear.

EUPATORIUM

Mithridates Eupator, a king of Pontus in the long ago, thought a certain species of this genus was antidote for poison—hence the name. It is often called, Hardy Ageratum, because the blooms look like this gentle little border annual. They are white, though, which one does not choose for Ageratum and the plant grows high, from four to five feet.

It succeeds anywhere and under almost any condition. Divides easily and seeds so freely that it is the part of discretion not to allow the flowerheads to ripen. Useful as a blender for any high growth. Blossoms in the fall.

GAILLARDIA

A plant which has been much improved during the last few years. From two to three feet high, the blossoms, which are like small sunflowers in form, appear by midsummer and continue till frost. They are gay things and the plant notable for its drought-resisting quality.

It will succeed in a poor soil but for perfection of bloom, give enrichment. It does not always come true from seed; an especially good variety should be increased by root-division in spring or from cuttings during the summer.

Named for the Frenchman, Gaillard, who was interested in botany. Popularly known as Blanket Flower.

The characteristic blossom is yellow tipped with red. Kelway's hybrids are especially good both for size of bloom and clearness of color.

HELENIUM

It has always seemed to me that this sturdy, tall-growing plant whose flower clusters appear in the fall, is misnamed. Helen's flower it is, and no less a Helen than she who was Queen of Troy. Now the Helenium is a useful, obliging creature, not a thing of exotic beauty and utterly lacking fragrance. Mind you, I like it and resent the common name, Sneezeweed. I only stress that it has no characteristic of its namesake.

Divides easily and may be grown in ordinary soil. The blossoms are borne at the top and, because of this and that it is a heavy bloomer, staking is a wise precaution.

H. autumnale, 3 to 5 feet high, has yellow flowers. A variety of this called Autumn Glow has blooms of yellow with undermarking of wallflower red.

Riverton Gem, 5 feet high, is yellow, which changes later to red; Riverton Beauty, 4 feet, is lemon yellow with a center of purple black.

Bigelovi, 4 feet, is a rich yellow with brown center.

HELIANTHUS

In English, this means Sunflower and to me at least, brings remembrance of the rugged, coarse-growing annual to be seen about all well-regulated farmhouses. Loved of birds for the seeds' sake, I venture to say that if it were difficult to grow, the gardener too would appreciate it more highly. Its decorative possibility is unrivaled. And yet, for all its admirable qualities, it is scarcely suited to the garden. This is not true of the perennials which, although they possess all the sturdiness of their better known relatives, have blooms which are not so overwhelming in size.

Ordinary soil is better than enrichment, which makes them rank without apparent gain. Root-division is simple and almost invariably successful, which is fortunate because they are so late coming into bloom that seeds sometimes do not have time to ripen. As the name implies, give full sun.

H. Maximiliani is tall, 8 feet at least, and late in flowering. H. lætiflorus is shorter, blooms earlier and is a brighter yellow.

This name has been given to other flowers and the various stories to the effect that a bloom so called turns toward the sun is obviously not in reference to this particular one—the heavy stems, even in the most credulous times, could never have been expected to perform such miracle. As matter of fact, in this case, the name is descriptive of the appearance of the bloom.

HELIOPSIS

Another sturdy plant of fall flowering called, literally, sunlike because it wears His Majesty's color and form. It is also known as Hardy Zinnia; the blooms are not unlike. Blossoms earlier than Helianthus, sometimes by July, and is shorter, about 3 feet.

Increase by division or seed and grow in ordinary soil.

INULA

Still another plant with yellow, Marguerite-like blooms. The name is said to be a corruption of Helenium. The life habit of this less known and slightly inferior relative is similar—easy root-division, ordinary soil. Sometimes called Fleabane.

The species I. Helenium (Elecampane) is prized by the French because Vin d'Aulnée is made from it.

LEONTOPODIUM

From leon, the lion, and pous, a foot, because of the shape; the wee flowerets are like the pads of this King of the Jungle. These grow in close clusters surrounded by a rosette of whitish woolly bracts. A curious rather than beautiful flower, you may be saying.

Wait! Let me tell you its other name and you will admit it gladly to your rock-garden if for no better reason than that of association. It is the Edelweiss, that witch-growth to be found between chinks in the rocks high up in the Alps, to pick which the mountaineer will risk life itself.

One might thing with reason that anything with such a history might be difficult to tame. This is not fact, for it may be grown for the home rockery from seed and asks nothing unusual in way of soil.

There is a tale of its origin worth remembering. An angel grew weary of heaven and longed to re-visit the earth. Permission was given her to take the form of a mortal maid. As might be expected, she found herself ill-adjusted to human contact and so chose to live in the eerie wildness of an Alpine peak where she was able to look upon the things of earth and yet remain apart.

One day, a daring climber caught sight of her. Soon the fame of this strange Snow Maiden lured many another to the heights. Her beauty doomed all who saw to hopeless love; for it was her fate to remain ever cold. Her lovers in despair begged that they be relieved from her spell, so she was called back to heaven. As remembrance of her visit to earth, her heart remains forever in the Edelweiss.

LIATRIS

Brilliant of color, the Liatris, as the popular names, Gay Flower and Blazing Star, would indicate. Easy to grow too, and natives of North America. Their tall spikes of bloom continue from midsummer till frost and have the rather unusual habit of opening first from the top of the stalk.

Hardy and easily increased by division in the spring. To succeed with seeds however, sow as soon as they ripen.

L. pycnostachya, from 4 to 5 feet high, the best known species, is also called, Kansas Gay Flower. The bloom-spikes of bright purple seem to have unusual attraction for butterflies. L. spicata is quite similar; a bit shorter and slightly earlier in flowering.

PYRETHRUM

Painted Daisy, is the popular name for this charming plant; best of those with the daisy-form. It has all the virtues. Strong yet slender of stem, of keeping quality, it is especially good as a cut flower; the foliage is dainty and, if after the time of heavy bloom—June, the spent stalks be cut away, still remains an ornament which, occasionally, will give a second blooming in the fall; easy of culture in ordinary soil; may be divided in spring or grown from seed.

You may have it in white, pink, rose or red—pink preferably: double or single. In this instance I depart from my prejudice and recommend the doubles.

The name comes from pur, fire, because of the acrid taste of the roots.

STOKESIA

Stokes' Aster! Named for the English botanist, Stokes and to his honor. Called by some Cornflower Aster, which will tell the initiate of its perfect blue. From a foot to a foot and a half in height, blooming from June to late October.

Species S. cyanea is best in color, although those who ask variety may include S. cyanea cœrulea, a lighter blue, or even S. cyanea alba, a white. Foliage of them all, a rich green, good for cutting.

Increased by division in spring, from cuttings after bloom, or seeds. Although not imperative, a sandy loam, best for growing.

As matter of fact, better when treated as an annual, which means that seed should be taken each year—just in case.

TANACETUM

Species vulgare, variety crispum (referring to the curled leaves) is a cut-leaf form of the common Tansy—famed for tea of a sort. For such a common creature, it is not surprising to find that division is simple, cuttings invariably successful, seeds readily germinated.

As matter of candor, the foliage is superior to the blooms which are usually cut off when it is used as a carpeting.

The origin of the name is obscure and may have possible romance—there is certainly no other to be found for the plant.

THE CRASSULACEÆ

The Houseleeks, and easily recognized by succulent leaves, often gray-green. Usually low of growth and with showy flowers. As a whole the family delights in dry, hot, exposed locations. Species native to the United States come from the western coast.

SEDUM

SEMPERVIVUM

SEDUM

Sedum, often called Stonecrop, is named from sedere, to sit, because it clings so closely to stone as to seem to be sitting upon it. Surely, anything which can take ease on such uncomfortable material should never be denied the privilege. Low, creeping growth for the most part, it has many uses outside the rockery; odd niches in walls, stonework or flagging may be softened by it—the fleshy leaves makes it able to withstand an extremely dry location.

It is easily increased because the smallest particle will root. I have often snipped a bit and set it in a spot where I have wished a new plant, although I am frank to admit that this is lazy gardening.

S. acre has moss-like leaves and inconspicuous yellow blooms; S. album, a bit larger leaves and loose white flowerheads borne on stiff stems slightly raised above the foliage. A less interesting species, S. aizoon, still larger leaves and heads of yellow bloom on fleshy stems. S. lydium has bronzy foliage with pink bloom; this and S. glaucum, glaucous-green of foliage, make choice rock-garden subjects. There are other good species.

The aristocrat of the genus is S. spectabile with gray spoon-shaped leaves and blossoms of large rose flowerheads. This is often used as a pot-plant and grows from one to two feet high. It flowers in September and is one of the graces of the old garden in Marblehead, where it is used extensively as an edging.

SEMPERVIVUM

The quite obvious meaning of the name is, to live forever, and not given as in the case of the so-called "Everlastings" because the bloom may be cut for winter bouquets; rather that the genus is tenacious of life and may be comfortable in almost desert condition of aridity. Rich diet and coddling do not please it so well. It is also called, Houseleek, for the very good reason that it will grow on the mellowed wood of old houses. A pleasant sight it is when perched saucily on the cottager's thatched roof.

There are several species and those who have a liking for the unusual in gardening have been known to tuck a collection in some out of the way corner. The three most acceptable for general gardening are S. tectorum, the Roof-leek; S. globiferum, named for shape; S. arachnoideum, which starts as a single rosette of leaves and develops by throwing other, smaller rosettes around the parent—a habit which has earned it the descriptive name, Hen and Chickens. They are as easy to increase as Sedums, and although the blooms are not quite so good, the leaf mosaics are more interesting.

In the days when thunder was thought as dangerous as it sounds, Sempervivum was supposed to be a protection from it. We learn that the great Charlemagne commanded his subjects to set it on their roofs. So you see, this little plant may be rightly considered the true forerunner of the lightning-rod.

THE CRUCIFERÆ

A large family with all the blooms marked by a Greek cross, which is responsible for the name, cross-bearers.

They are to be found in all countries, yet have a preference for the temperate zone. There are useful members such as cabbage, turnip, radish, mustard, cress, horse-radish, as well as many charming flowers.

ÆTHIONEMA
ALYSSUM
ARABIS
AUBRIETIA
CHIERANTHUS (*Wallflower*)
DRABA
IBERIS (*Candytuft*)

ÆTHIONEMA

A rock plant from 6 to 12 inches high, forming compact little bushes. Stems woody, foliage blue-green, blooms, rose, and borne on racemes from June to July.

The name, from aitho, to scorch and nema, a filament, refers to the burnt appearance of the stamens.

It is a bit difficult to establish and prefers a stony, sandy loam in full sun. Better for a slight cutting back after bloom. Do not risk root-division; cuttings after bloom or seeds are safer.

ALYSSUM

Everyone who gardens grows annual Alyssum; it is a delightful necessity. The perennial is not invariably included in a planting, yet might well be to the garden's greater glory. A rockery is the better for it and would be if there were no bloom—foliage of gray is ever welcome, there or for edging.

Full sun and lime in the soil are its preference. Increase by division or seed.

A. saxatile, var. compactum, called, Basket of Gold, from 8 to 12 inches high, bears yellow flowers in profusion during the spring. A. argenteum, a dwarf, is still earlier of bloom and continues the good habit throughout the season. The leaves are silver underneath which is reason for the name.

From a, not and lyssa, rage, because of the belief that it soothes anger. Sometimes called, Madwort: is this promise or threat?

ARABIS

A creeper and from Arabia, an arid land which makes possible that this alien may grow under like condition. The blooms of white come early and are not so much; the leaf rosettes, on the contrary are nice at any time.

If you wish to increase, and you should, just cut these. Roots form often before they have promise of soil.

To keep this edging trim, divide; otherwise it becomes straggly.

AUBRIETIA

Early of bloom and with the nice habit—for the rockery at least, of creeping. Foliage, gray-green, flowers, lilac to purple with the cross characteristic of the family strongly marked.

Any good soil; may be increased by seeds, from cuttings of non-flowering stalks, or pegging.

Named for M. Aubrient, a French artist.

CHEIRANTHUS

Commonly called Wallflower because it takes kindly to this location in a warmish climate. The scientific name, from cheir, hand, and anthos, flower, was given for its popularity when used in nosegays. This was corrupted by Chaucer to cherisaunce. As is inevitable for blossom of such delightful fragrance, it has acquired other names, among them, Heart's Ease, Wall Violet, Winter Gilliflower.

A favorite with troubadours and knights of old who wore it in the cap when about to sally forth for deeds of adventure. I have already told of its place in legend (The Annuals Of Flowerland, page 45). Let me stress what I said there about its dislike of cold winters. Better treat as a biennial, that is, grow from seed each year. Sow in the coldframe not later than July and keep the plants there during the first winter—it transplants easily.

C. Allioni, one foot high is best in the rockery: C. cheiri, the type, is taller and charming among plants of medium height in the border. Both prefer rich soil mixed with a little sand.

DRABA

For the rockery. In a sunny, warm place and with ordinary soil, it grows in chinks and crevices of rock forming compact clumps. The yellow blooms are early and a popular name, Whitlow Grass, is evidence of foliage value throughout the season.

The name is from drabe, acrid and refers to the juice. D. cuspidata and D. lasiocarpa (woolly-fruited and interesting because so), are good species.

IBERIS

Truth admits or should, that the annual forms are better. Still, there is one, I. sempervirens, another, I. gibraltarica, of the perennial sort, worthy place in any planting. Both are good as edgings; the first is covered by a mass of white bloom in the spring, the second, a pinkish white. The foliage of dark green makes cool contrast to hot bloom or hot weather throughout the season.

Ordinary soil. So easy to divide or make cuttings that to increase from seed is unnecessary.

Named Iberia because its home land is Spain, which was called Iberia in the classic world.

NOTES

Truth admits, as should, that the annual forms are further still, there is [illegible] illustration of the perennial [illegible] planted [illegible] covered by a mass of white [illegible] splendid white. The foliage [illegible] makes [illegible] contrast [illegible] throughout the season.

Ordinarily [illegible] may be [illegible] or make [illegible] that [illegible].

Named Iberis, because [illegible] land of Spain, which was called Iberia in the ancient world.

THE DIPSACEÆ

Small blooms growing in clusters and opposite leaves are simple identification marks for this family. You may object that this is also true of many Composites, and you will be perfectly right. The difference between the two families lies in the anthers, which with the Dipsaceæ are longer and raised above the other organs of the flower.

SCABIOSA (*Pincushion Flower*)

SCABIOSA

It may be a personal experience, my hope that it is, to find the annual Scabiosas easier to germinate than the perennials.

The perennials are so worth while, especially, S. caucisica, 18 inches high, light blue of bloom and flowering from June to October; strong in stem, too, making a perfect cut flower: S. japonica, 2 feet, with blossoms of blue-lavender, later to bloom, more often than one would wish, September.

Ordinary soil and increased by seed or division in spring.

The name is unpleasant, coming from scabies, the itch, because it is said to cure. Pincushion Flower or Mourning Bride are far more suited.

THE EUPHORBIACEÆ

A useful family, especially outside the flower-garden. It gives to those who desire such, cascarilla, croton-oil and castor-oil and, although most abundant in South America, is to be found in both temperate and tropical zones. The Croton and Poinsettia are members from the south, while two annual species of the genus Euphorbia, E. heterophylla (Fire-on-the-Mountain) and E. variegata (Snow-on-the-Mountain) serve useful purpose in northern gardens wherever something gay and yet unexacting as to soil and moisture is required.

All members have milky juice and inconspicuous flowers: it is the colorful leaves and bracts which give the high note.

EUPHORBIA (*Spurge*)

EUPHORBIA

For the most part, native of South America, yet named for Euphorbus, physician to a king of Mauritania. Sometimes called Spurge, oftener, Milkwort, because of the milky juice which exudes from any broken part.

Although the annuals are gayer—note Poinsettia, Fire-on-the-Mountain, Snow-on-the-Mountain, there are worthwhile perennials. E. corollata, 1 to 1½ feet high, not unlike Gypsophila and as such fine in combination with other flowers and blooming from July to late August. E. polychroma, 2 feet, early in spring; chrome-yellow.

Light, rich soil and mix in a bit of lime. The blossoms of annual and perennial alike are inconspicuous; it is the bracts which are showy.

THE GENTIANACEÆ

A smallish family, although widely distributed. Gentian, its typical genus, is welcome wherever it will grow for the gorgeous blue of most species. Isn't it a fact that when we wish to cite blue supreme, we never give thought to the various new names coined by certain purveyors of fashion? We know the ultimate word to be "Gentian blue."

GENTIANA

GENTIANA

"Blue—blue—as if that sky let fall
A flower from its cerulean wall."

Called for Gentius, King of Illyria, who thought it remedy for poison, pestilence, bite of mad dog, lameness, or that lesser evil, indigestion.

Another kingly person, one Ladislaw of Hungary, when his domain was stricken with a plague, graciously consented to find a cure. According to the imperfect science of his time, he believed that wherever an arrow shot from the royal bow might fall, a remedy would be found. It hit a plant of Gentian and since that day, this has been considered of medicinal value.

The plant prefers moisture and a sandy loam with half shade. G. Andrewii, one to two feet high, a native of the United States, is the Closed or Bottled Gentian. G. crinita is that delight of the poet, Fringed Gentian. Both have blooms of deepest blue and are late in flowering. G. macrophylla (with large leaves) is only a foot high and has pale blue blossoms in July.

THE HYPERICACEÆ

A small family containing a few trees, some shrubs and herbs, also annuals and perennials, although most of these are not sufficiently decorative for the garden. The leaves of all forms of growth are usually simple and opposite and the flowers either yellow or white with five sepals, generally five petals and many stamens.

HYPERICUM

HYPERICUM

From yper, on account of, and ereike, heath: it will grow in windy, exposed places like the Heath. Also called St. John's Wort, and thereby hangs a tale. Certain missionaries went to a cold country and found the plant there. They gave it wholesome consecration because of its courage, and since that time it is supposed to act as a guardian from witches. If a sprig be hung over the door on that frolic time of the unpleasant creatures, Walpurgis night or the eve of St. John, it gives protection. The mountaineers of the Tyrol hold for fact that a bit of it placed in the shoe will rob climbing of fatigue.

A tiny plant to be so potent and, therefore, best in the rockery. You may have H. hyssopifolium, four inches, with blueish foliage and cup-shaped blooms of yellow; H. orientale, slightly taller and flowering in clusters; H. polyphyllum, a paler yellow. Ordinary soil. Easy to divide.

ERYNGIUM

[illegible], on account of [illegible] [illegible]. [illegible] it will grow in sandy, exposed places like the Heath. Also called sea-holly. [illegible] and [illegible] brings a tale. Certain [illegible] went to a cold country and found the plant there. They gave it [illegible] [illegible] because of [illegible], [illegible] that time it is supposed to act as a guardian from [illegible]. It ought to be hung over the door to ward [illegible] of the [illegible] [illegible]. [illegible] [illegible] of the [illegible] of St. John [illegible] [illegible]. The [illegible] of the [illegible] hold for [illegible] a [illegible] [illegible] planted in the same with [illegible] of [illegible].

A dry plant in [illegible] and [illegible]. [illegible]. You may have [illegible] [illegible] inches [illegible] and cup-shaped blooms of yellow; E. [illegible], slightly taller and flowering in [illegible]; E. [illegible], a pale yellow. Ordinary soil. May be divide.

THE IRIDACEÆ

Perhaps this family is best represented by bulbs; for without it our gardens would be the poorer for lack of the Gladiolus, the Crocus, the Ixia, to say nothing of many beautiful bulbous Iris.

When we learn that it is most abundant on the shores of the Mediterranean and in South Africa, it is understandable that some members are tender in the temperate zone. Herbaceous Iris, fortunately is hardy, be it wee or giant, and enriches the border by sword-like foliage and, during the period of bloom, rare and lovely color. As matter of fact, some of the color-combinations are so startling that only Mother Nature herself could carry them to success.

IRIS

IRIS

Blossomland would lose much if there were no Iris. Named for the rainbow, it wears all her colors. Charming in all its forms, from the wildling of the meadow (I. versicolor) and others of sturdy beauty which grow for cottage or castle alike, to the few aristocrats which must be given especial care.

It is divided into two groups: the bulbous, such as the Spanish and English types, and the herbaceous. Because I have from necessity excluded from the pages of this book all growth which is not from perennial roots, only the second group may be considered. As matter of fact, to give this its due would mean many pages. Varieties are legion. Once you begin to grow Iris, you will grow more; possibly join an Iris Society; certainly fall under the spell of the plant's fascinating ways.

All I shall attempt is a brief mention of the various kinds and add a recommendation to try them all. First in importance is the Bearded or Germans—this because they are hardy and require little in way of attention. They prefer ordinary soil, need little moisture and may be divided at any time by method so careless as to seem butchery. Yet they are generous of bloom and in shape so exotic as to have been called the Poor Man's Orchid. The flowering period is short, yet, if one choose both early and late varieties, it will carry through the first six weeks of spring.

For colors, go to the nurseryman's catalogue. There is a wide choice. One caution—do not plant deep, merely cover the roots.

From the standpoint of hardiness, I. florentina comes next. It blooms later than I. germanica, is taller, and the flowers are slightly scented. The colors are light, usually a blending of white with lavender or pale blue. I. siberica is shorter and a bit less hardy. It may be yellow, blue or white; contrasting colors will seldom be found in this species. Both like a moist soil.

I. kaempferi (Japanese Iris) is the finest of all for size of bloom. It requires a heavy, moist soil and, to be at its best, extra enrichment after the buds have formed. Buy named varieties. It does not take kindly to transplanting; division should be made carefully in the late fall. It is better not to cultivate till after blooming time.

Then, there are a certain few suited to the rockery; wee things with flowers two or three inches high and coming in the spring. For the gardener who does not specialize in Iris culture, I. cristata, light blue, and I. plumila, purple, yellow or white, will be sufficient for this purpose.

Set all Iris in the fall.

Probably you all know that the Lily which was the emblem of royal France was the Fleur de Lis, an Iris.

THE LABIATÆ

A large and important family which may be identified by its square stems. It is named from the lip-shaped corolla of the flowers.

This is often called the Mint Family and is especially useful for savories; spearmint, peppermint, catmint, rosmary, basil, marjoram and sage are members. Also that cleanest and most wholesome fragrance, lavender.

AJUGA
LAVANDULA (*Lavender*)
MONARDA
PHYSOSTEGIA
SALVIA (*Sage*)
STACHYS (*Lamb's Tongue*)
THYMUS

AJUGA

One of those humble plants which earn respect because of amiable disposition. A. reptans, a creeper, is called Bugleweed—Bugle, because of the shape of the tiny deep blue blooms and weed because it will grow in common soil with no attention whatsoever; under dry condition, under wet condition; in shade, even under trees where grass would not succeed. Cuttings will root at any time.

The botanical name is from a, not, and zugon, a yoke, because the calyx is one-leaved.

LAVANDULA

Lavandula is more readily recognized by its English name, Lavender. The word comes from lavo, to wash. Especially appropriate, isn't it, when we recall those chests of hand-woven linen fragrant with the purity of its dried blossoms? Even in this day, when heavy perfume is the mode, the charms of Lavender lingers.

L. vera is the species which is grown for fragrance. This should by no means be exiled to the herb garden. Its leaves of whitish gray are delightful in the border and the flowers of blue quite as welcome there as in the boudoir.

It grows from 2 to 3 feet high and prefers loam mixed with a little sand. Give slight winter protection and increase by cuttings of the non-flowering shoots.

MONARDA

Although all the Monardas are native to North America, they were named for Dr. Monardez, a physician of Seville during the period of its splendor.

M. didyma, growing from 2 to 3 feet high, is a good garden subject, provided one has place for red there. It is aromatic rather than fragrant and is often called Bee Balm, because of its fascination for these garden friends. A sturdy thing which will grow in common soil and under any condition save deep shade. It increases rapidly and may be divided at any time. Blooms in June.

PHYSOSTEGIA

The plant grows about three feet high and the foliage, although small, is rather coarse in texture. It flowers in September; spikes of light pink blooms which look like wee bladders (the name, from phusa, a bladder and stege, a covering, is because of this.)

It prefers partial shade, rich soil and moisture. If the season is dry, water liberally just before flowering time. One of the few plants which is better for frequent transplanting. It may be increased by cuttings of the young shoots, root-division in spring or by seed. Seedlings reach blooming earlier than is usual with perennials.

P. virginica, is the species usually grown; variety, alba of course, is white. A new variety, Vivid, has larger individual blooms and flowers later than the type. All are good for cutting because of keeping quality.

SALVIA

He, little Salvia, knows who thinks of it in terms of S. splendens, that flaming annual about which I have already expressed myself unpleasantly—(Annuals Of Flowerland, p. 77). The aristocrats of the genus are perennials; so too is the commonest, S. officinalis (Sage of the pungent personality).

I make amend for my prejudice against S. splendens by the fact that the perennials are given high honor in my garden—especially S. azurea, var. grandiflora. Its gray leaves always give cool contrast and when in August, that hottest of months, light blue flowers appear, they heighten this welcome effect. In rich soil it grows from 3 to 4 feet high. Unfortunately, the stems are weak, making some sort of support necessary.

S. argentea is a bit lower, with yellow flowers in June; S. patens, 2 feet, with deep blue blooms in September; S. pitcheri, sometimes called Meadow Sage, is the darkest blue and flowers late.

Give rich soil and increase by root-division. The name comes from salvo, to save, because of a reputed medicinal quality.

STACHYS

S. lanata, called Lamb's Tongue, because of the shape and texture of the leaves. An excellent border plant for the large garden; it is a bit too coarse and vigorous of growth for such purpose where space is a consideration. The blossoms (July) borne on thick stems above the foliage, are of light lavender and, it must be admitted, rather unimpressive. There are those who cut them away—a custom which I deplore—they are good to blend with finer flower indoors. Yet, even a friend of the plant must acknowledge that it is the leaves of silvery gray which give it place in a planting.

Increase by division is so easy as to make seed-sowing absurd—especially when frequent cutting is imperative lest it become too aggressive. Will grow in any soil.

The botanical name is from stachus, a spike.

THYMUS

"I know a bank," said one who is never wrong. For Thymus, or Thyme, is an outlaw to be grown as carpeting or between rocks and paving stones. Yet its aromatic leaves are delightful. Not a creeper, as is the way with most growth of this sort; it is sometimes two feet high.

The flowers are purple and increase may be made by seeds, cuttings or division. It will prosper in poor soil—in fact under any soil condition.

The name is from thuo, to perfume.

THE LEGUMINOSÆ

A huge family with butterfly-shaped blooms and fruits which are called legumes, and responsible for the family name. There are especially lovely trees, the Locusts, the Judas Tree, and the Coffee Tree of the South (called thus because the early settlers of Kentucky used its seeds as a substitute for the coffee berry). Also the more tender Acacias and Minosas.

And certainly such useful dwellers in the kitchen garden as the bean and pea should never go unmentioned.

BAPTISIA
CORONILLA
LATHYRUS
LUPINUS
THERMOPSIS

BAPTISIA

When Baptisia is first placed in the garden, either seedling or plant from the nurseryman, it may seem disappointing. The finely cut, dark green foliage will be pleasing throughout the season, but in all probability for a year or two, there will be no bloom. This is because the plant is slow to establish. On the other hand, its life is a long one.

When fully grown it is from two to two and a half feet high and in midsummer bears pea-like blooms of indigo blue. Once it reaches maturity it will send up side shoots which may be separated from the parent to make new plants. Ordinary soil and full sun.

B. australis is best for color. The name is from bapto, to dye, because B. tinctoria was used as a dye.

CORONILLA

This is not an especially valuable plant, in fact, might be classed as an "unloved flower" or weed. In addition, the only species sufficiently attractive for garden use, C. varia, has poisonous juice. The flowers of pink and white are pea-shaped. Perhaps its one reason for place in Flowerland is that it will bear any amount of neglect—and this is a virtue to one who wishes green-growing things and has little time to care for them.

Ordinary soil; easy to increase from seed or cutting. The name means a crown or garland because the blossoms grow in this form.

LATHYRUS

Lathyrus latifolius, the Everlasting Pea, like its more delicate relative, Sweet Pea, is in reality a climber. The tendrils which end the leaf-midribs show that. Still with a bit of support, it is useful in the garden. A sturdy creature and, because so, the support may be removed at any time allowing the growth to cover spots made vacant by plant of ephemeral growth. I place it near Delphinium; it is nice as a filler between first and second blooming. A few plants grown among Sweet Peas will give the whole an appearance of stability; it will withstand heat which would be fatal to its more aristocratic sister.

There are two varieties, Pink Beauty, not an overly successful pink, and White Pearl—far better. Either, when cut and arranged with gray-green leaves is delightful. To compensate in part for the lack of fragrance, they possess the virtue of keeping quality.

Although not necessary, rich soil stimulates growth. To increase by seed is the best method—it self-seeds. The name is from la, to add to, and thouros, an irritant, because the seeds of certain species not so much add as cause this.

LUPINUS

Called for lupus, the wolf, because a certain wild species is so wolfish of nature as to kill everything nearby. The garden sort, to the contrary, is a gentle creature with never an aggressive habit—one might wish it more. From infancy to old age it is welcome because of foliage. And when June comes, bringing flowers, it is unforgettable. The spikes of bloom, three feet high, may be white, blue or rose and in a new strain, called Regal, shades of amber, coppery orange, yellow, bronze, rose, terra-cotta, slate, lavender. L. polyphyllus, a native of California, is the species from which this wonder variety comes.

The plant should have a warm, sunny place and is easily increased by seed or division. Seedlings grow quickly and blossom at an age earlier than usual with perennials; under favorable condition, the first season.

There is a misunderstanding as to soil condition. Some folk—I incline to think, inexperienced folk, still hold the tradition that lime is fatal. This is not fact. Just remember that there should not be *excess* of lime. Rich soil is necessary for best development.

THERMOPSIS

From thermos, a Lupine and opsis, like, which describes it well. It grows somewhat higher than its prototype but is restricted to bloom of yellow which comes in June or July. T. caroliniana is the best garden species.

Increase by seed. Give ordinary soil.

THE LILIACEÆ

Although the genus Lilium may not be admitted to this book on herbaceous perennials because it is bulbous, there are many of its lovely relatives—all more or less lily-like in appearance which make any book or garden more desirable. Leaves, for the most part, are lance-like although there are some exceptions. Among the herbaceous perennials, white and yellow are the prevailing blossom colors with an occasional pink. The bulbous members, Tulip and Hyacinth are among them, and carry all the colors of the rainbow.

The family is distributed over the world and a delight wherever met. Even the humble onion is pleasing to the eye, you know!

ASPHODELUS
EREMURUS
FUNKIA
HEMERCALLIS (*Yellow Day lily*)
POLYGONATUM (*Solomon's Seal*)
TRILLIUM
UVULARIA (*Bellwort*)
YUCCA (*Adam's Needle*)

ASPHODELUS

The botanical name which is usually Englished to Asphodel, is from a, not and spallo, to supplant; this because of its striking appearance. The popular name, King's Spear, suggests further its characteristic growth form.

It thrives in ordinary garden soil and with enrichment reaches a height of four feet. A. lutea, is the finest. Erect in form with dark green leaves which are especially handsome because of lighter veinings. In midsummer, terminal spikes of fragrant yellow blooms give added beauty.

EREMURUS

How well I remember my first sight of an Eremurus root! It came in a box of plants I had ordered and was protected from the others by a wire netting. A note of warning that it should be given careful handling was attached. When I lifted it from a bed a spagnum, I understood why caution was necessary—the fleshy, curiously-formed thing looked like an octapus. Judged by eye alone, it would seem tough. As matter of fact, it is easily broken and the plant sensitive to this. A native of Asia, in cooler climate it requires winter protection. Further, it has the unpleasant habit of dying down to the roots after bloom.

You may think that I have made a poor case for Eremurus. This is not my wish: I have grown it successfully for years. If given a sunny place and rich sandy loam, it will reach at least eight feet. Before blooming time be sure that it gets plenty of water.

It develops seeds only during a hot summer and these are slow to germinate, sometimes requiring two years. They should be planted as soon as ripe. E. robustus, a light pink, is the hardiest—perhaps I should say, the least fragile. When the regal spikes of bloom appear in June, you will, I hope, agree with me that extra care is worthwhile.

The name is from eremos, solitary and oura, a tail, in description of the flowering stalks.

FUNKIA

The genus is named for a German botanist, H. Funk. It is popularly known as Plantain Lily because of the broad, deeply veined leaves above which the flower-stalks are lifted. All species like rich, well-drained soil and have the merit of growing equally well in sun or shade. They may be divided either in the fall or spring; perhaps spring is the better time.

F. subcordata, often called White Daylily, not only has the finest blooms (white and sweetly scented) but is the most useful. If not divided, it reaches shrub proportion and makes a useful hedging where anything dense and about two feet high is needed. It blooms from late July through a good part of August.

F. lancifolia has narrower leaves and, in August, smaller blossoms of light lavender. F. l. var. variegata has striking green and white foliage and purple flowers—these are not especially attractive; many gardeners cut them away and use the plant as an edging.

HEMEROCALLIS

Literally, day beauty, because each bloom lives for only one day. Several are borne on the strong, stiff stalks and, if brought indoors, the buds will open there. As might be expected of a plant with such habit, it likes partial shade, although full sunshine does no injury. It will grow in ordinary soil and may be divided either in spring or fall

The lance-like leaves are good throughout the garden year and, by selecting different species, the flowering season may be carried from June to September. All kinds are yellow and some of the lighter ones, delightfully fragrant.

Probably everyone knows H. fulva, the tall Orange Lily of the roadside. It is considered rather coarse for the garden; there are those who banish it entirely. Still at the back, if a bit of strong gayety is wanted, it is not out of place. The flowering stalks are three feet high. H. flava, the Lemon Daylily, which blossoms in June, is welcome anywhere, as is H. thunbergi, very similar but blooming much later—August or September. Both are about two feet high. H. middendorffi, a deeper yellow, flowers over a longer season. It is from two to two and a half feet high.

POLYGONATUM

The botanical name, from polys, many, and gonu, a joint, was given because of the joints on the stems and the popular name, Solomon's Seal, for a far nicer reason—after the leaf and flower stems fall, there is a roundish, depressed scar left on the creeping root-stalk.

As matter of fact, all Polygonatums are woodsy wildlings. Yet P. multiflorum is amenable to garden condition. In rich soil it will grow two or three feet high and has a decided preference for shade. It is nice under trees or in a shaded part of the border. The greenish-white blossoms, growing in racemes, are inconspicuous. They come in June and are followed in the fall by more interesting blue-black berries.

Both flower and foliage keep exceptionally well when cut.

TRILLIUM

Well named, from trilix, triple, because all the floral parts are in threes. Often called Wood Lily, and native to North America. It *must* be given shade, a well-drained soil of leaf mold mixed with a little sand; plenty of moisture. Divide as well as plant in autumn.

T. grandiflorum (May) has snowy-white flowers, sometimes three inches across. The plant is from a foot to a foot and a half in height and the foliage is good some time after the bloom has passed. T. undulatum or erythocarpum, is the beautiful Painted Trillium, native of cool, damp woods and hard to grow elsewhere. Still, if set deep, kept moist and away from the sun's direct rays, it sometimes adapts itself to other condition. It is worth any trouble—the spring offers nothing lovelier.

UVULARIA

Called so because of a supposed medicinal help to the uvula. Native to North America and very hardy. U. grandiflora is the only species suitable for garden purpose. From one to two feet high with smooth oblong leaves. The yellow blooms are bell-shaped—called Bellwort because of this. They open before leaves have fully developed.

Give a light sandy loam and divide in spring.

YUCCA

In the tropics, Yuccas are used principally for hedging; the sharp-toothed, swordlike leaves are admirable for such purpose. It is an arresting sight when the tall stalks of bell-like blooms flower above them. Even in England it is classed as an evergreen shrub.

In the temperate parts of North America it must be considered a perennial and, because of this, the foliage has less the quality of cactus growth; the bloom stalks too are lower—about four feet. Y. filamentosa, with blossoms of soft white, is the species most commonly grown. Give a sandy loam and increase by suckers from the roots.

Yucca is suitable only for the large garden. It is often called Adam's Needle. Just why, one wonders. There is no historic evidence that the gentleman was either domestic or a giant. The name comes from Peru.

THE LINACEÆ

The family, a small one, is of value chiefly as herbs. The most important and largest genus, Linum, which includes all the Flaxes, is unusual, botanically, in that all floral organs—sepals, petals, stamens and pistils, are five in number. The leaves are narrow and in some species the fiber, very strong.

LINUM (*Flax*)

LINUM

From linon, flax, and commonly called by that name.

L. perenne, the only perennial species sufficiently attractive and sufficiently hardy to find universal welcome, is a native of England where it is an evergreen. With us, it is herbaceous and from one to one and a half feet high. Its slender leaves are charming and, if given sufficient space for symmetrical development, becomes a thing of grace throughout the season. During June and July, flowers of pale blue cover it. L. perenne, var. alba, is, of course, a white form of the same plant.

It likes a rich soil and is easily raised from seed. Division in spring is possible, although cuttings after blossom-time is the safer method.

In German folklore, sacred to Hilda, the goddess of plenty.

THE MALVACEÆ

The blooms of this large family are strikingly handsome, in fact some of those native to the temperate zones seem so exotic that it is pleasant surprise to find the plants hardy. Without benefit of hybridizer the colors are purple, a hard rose or yellow. Happily nature aided by science has improved on this.

A family unusual in that it has no poisonous or even unwholesome members—most of the blossoms look good enough to eat were they not too beautiful to despoil.

Various parts of many species are used medicinally. The cotton plant is greatest in economic importance.

ALTHÆA ROSEA (*Hollyhock*)
HIBISCUS
MALVA (*Musk Mallow*)
SIDALCEA

ALTHÆA ROSEA

From altheo, to cure, in reference to the medicinal quality of some species. The genus contains both perennials and biennials and is of priceless value to the garden because of one biennial—Althæa rosea, the parent and still the botanical name of Hollyhock.

A perennial this, in its native China, and although it flourished three centuries ago, even then apparently, was as tall and with the rough-heart-shaped leaves of our modern varieties. The difference—such a difference!—was that all flowers were pink and smallish.

Now one may choose from any color, almost any shade of any color with the exception of blue; white also: blooms single or double, the doubles forming rosettes of such silky loveliness as to seem preferable. Borne on regal stalks in midsummer. For the fastidious, there are always new and named varieties at little added cost. And no matter how humble the variety, Hollyhock never disappoints.

Rich soil, plenty of moisture, good drainage suits it best. Increased easily by seed, although this is one of nature's gambles; they seldom come true. Division of root-stock—the one sure method to duplicate color, is possible, although not easy.

HIBISCUS

Named by none other than Vergil. Marsh Mallow, the popular name, suggests bog moisture; yet a few species are sufficiently obliging as to grow without such.

To know this plant in its splendor one must go to the tropics, where shrub species give blooms of gorgeous color the year through.

H. moscheutos is kind and will bear its huge flowers, either white or pink, and purple of center, in cooler climate. Do not look for them till late summer.

Rich soil, full sun. Increase by seeds or cuttings.

MALVA

Called Musk Mallow because of a musky fragrance; called Malva from malacho, to soften—it has emollient property. A native of Britain, two feet in height.

The flowers of rose, two inches across, are borne in terminal clusters, midsummer. Variety alba, with blooms of white is far lovelier.

Ordinary soil. Increase by seeds or root-division in spring.

SIDALCEA

From the Greek words, side, strength, and alkea, another. It is probable that *side* was the name of another Mallow which this resembles.

The plant is branching in form, from 2 to 3 feet high. Variety, Rose Queen, with rose-pink flowers in July and August, is the best. Contrary to the habit of the genus, the stamens are clustered in a central bundle.

Ordinary soil, sunny location, plenty of water. Although perennial, it is well to take seed: it's none too hardy. Seedlings are better than cuttings and those sown in late autumn produce stronger plants than from earlier bloom.

THE ONAGRACEÆ

Fragrance is a flower's greatest gift. A wise mortal willingly grants that this was not given merely to pleas-sure him. Still—he may enjoy!

Is it recognition of this stirring fact that although this family is composed for the most part of day-blooming members without fragrance, *it is known as Family Evening Primrose because of the unforgettable scent of the few which open after sunset?*

ŒNOTHERA (*Evening Primrose*)

ŒNOTHERA

From oinos, wine and thera, imbibing, because the root of a certain species was alleged to stimulate this worthy habit. Known as Primrose, term of enchantment which when "Evening" is added lifts to magic.

As sad fact, it must be admitted that the perennials do not live quite up to such merit. They are yellow for the most part—and white is good magic.

Choose from them if you will and wisely, O. Fraseri, rich yellow; O. Lamarkiana, lesser yellow; O. Missouriensis of the trailing stem, yellow too.

All like well drained soil, bettered for sand or gravel and, strange for such name, full sun. Increase by seed or division in spring.

THE PAPAVERACEÆ

BOCCONIA (*Plume Poppy*)
DICENTRA
PAPAVER (*Poppy*)
SANGUINARIA (*Bloodroot*)
MECONOPSIS

BOCCONIA

Named for Dr. P. Boccone, a Sicilian. Popularly called Plume Poppy: it looks much like a plume and little like a Poppy. B. cordata, a native of China, has strikingly handsome leaves, heart-shaped and blue-green. The spikes of cream colored flowers are followed by light brown seed-pods which are ornamental at the time when ornament is welcome.

In rich soil the plant often reaches twelve feet in height. An extremely hardy member of Flowerland: excellent as background and good for sunny corners. One bad habit must be told. It self-seeds too readily and in addition, the roots spread rapidly. So deal sternly with it lest it encroach on other growth.

DICENTRA

The name means two-spurred (di, twice, and kentron, a spur), given because of the spurs that end the petals, which are usually two in number. Lyre-shaped flowers are common to all species, also finely cut leaves and, alas, the fact that these disappear shortly after the flowering season. They require rich soil.

D. canadensis, called Squirrel Corn, is native of rich woods. It must have soil of the blackest (leaf mold is best) and moisture. This is not a plant for the garden save possibly, the rockery.

D. cucullaria (Dutchman's Breeches), and surely for a wee Dutchman, is another wood-loving creature. The foliage is so fairylike that it is cause of sincere regret that it dies soon. Still, there is always another spring! Both D. canadensis and cucullaria are best in the woods; although they may be brought into the rock-garden if given enrichment, shade and moisture.

D. eximia on the contrary makes an excellent edging. Eight inches is the average height and it spreads rapidly. The blooms are pink with a leaning to lavender and in common with other members of the genus, borne on racemes. There will be heavy bloom in June and July and light bloom throughout the season. It is an exception to the family's bad habit; the foliage does not disappear, although all that yellows should be cut away.

D. spectabilis is the tallest species, growing from two

to two and a half feet high; bushy in form. In May or June it bears many long racemes of heart-shaped flowers of bright pink. These are aptly described by the popular name, Bleeding Heart. It may be increased by seed, careful division, or root-cuttings, although I beg you not to sacrifice a well-established plant for root-cutting. Unfortunately, it has the family weakness and disappears after bloom. Its abiding-place should be marked, unobtrusively of course, lest it be injured. It does not take kindly to disturbance.

PAPAVER

Papaver, from papa, thick milk or pap, better known as that colorful necessity, the Poppy. There are two garden species which are perennial. P. nudicaule, known popularly as Iceland Poppy and P. orientale.

The foliage of P. nudicaule is gray-green and the blooms, an inch across, are lifted on slender stems above it. Heavy bloom in June and, if these are cut, slight bloom throughout the season. Probably you know that all Poppies should be cut as soon as color appears if you wish them for house decoration. Preëminently an Alpine and therefore excellent for the rockery, its cool green also makes excellent edging. It is permanent in congenial soil—rich and mixed with a little sand. Good drainage and full sunshine are necessary. As a matter of fact, it is a plant which needs a bit of coddling and, if you wish no anxiety during the winter as to what the spring may reveal, it is wise to sow seed in the coldframe—just in case. A buttercup yellow was the original color but the hybridizers have been especially successful in making new shades. Now, you may have a lighter or a deeper yellow, reddish orange, tangerine, the so-called "art shades," not forgetting white. Each year offers novelties.

P. orientale (Oriental Poppy) is the queen of them all; queen of the garden too when in bloom. Gorgeous flowers, from 6 to 8 inches across, are borne on thick stems, 2 to 3 feet long, the foliage of bright green grows in luxurious clumps. As soon as the blossoms have faded, the foliage should be cut down. Fill the vacant space with annuals from your reserve stock—all good gardeners have one, you know. Soon, new foliage will appear from the roots of Mme. Poppy and, occasionally, a second blooming. An orange-yellow is the type color of the Orientals. There are other and more lovely shades, such as Mrs. Perry, a salmon pink, or the flaming beauty called Royal Scarlet. It is well to look in several catalogues and annually for varieties; I venture to predict, in the matter of color, Oriental Poppy has a future.

There are many legends of Poppy, some of them sinister because of the scarlet of the common sort which came to typify blood. You may recall that the son of one of the Tarquins asked his father what should be the fate of a certain conquered city. The tyrant, instead of speaking, walked to a field of Poppies and slashed off the heads of the largest. The prominent citizens of the unfortunate town met a similar death.

There is another type of story because of P. somniferum, the opium bearer, which modern man in his folly has turned from blessing to curse. In the classic world. only the sleep-giving quality is stressed: this is the reason why it was supposed to grow about the couch of Somnos, god of sleep. And do you know why it flourishes near corn? It was this way. At the time when Prosephone, the daughter of Ceres, was stolen by Pluto, the mother made long and weary search for her throughout the island of Sicily, even climbing Mt. Ætna to light torches that she might continue the search throughout the night. The gods were powerless to bring back Prosephone and so, in pity for the harassed mother, caused Poppies to spring up about her feet. The blooms delighted her and she ate of the seeds which were so soothing that she slept. This is why the Poppy grows among the corn.

SANGUINARIA

Sanguinaria canadensis, called Bloodroot, is a plant of spring. In April, the leaves (oak-like in shape but gray-green) appear, followed shortly by blooms of so pure a whiteness as to seem reminiscent of the snow of the months before.

There are a few native wildlings which seem as indigenous to deep woods as a faun. This is one. Yet, it may be brought to the rockery if given woodland condition—that is, rich soil, shade, and moisture. The leaves are good till autumn and the creeping rootstalk is easily divided. It is especially effective when allowed to spread into a fairish clump. About 6 inches high.

The name means blood and was given because of the red sap.

MECONOPSIS

From mekon, the Greek word for Poppy and opsis, like, because of the appearance of the blossom.

M. cambrica (Welch Poppy), a native of the British Isles, is the best for color—a pale yellow. It is from a foot to a foot and a half in height and has the unpoppy-like virtue of continuous bloom. Give plenty of water and good drainage. It self-seeds so abundantly that one need not consider other method of increase.

THE PLUMBAGINEÆ

A small family of which several members are dry in texture and used as "everlastings." A few are herbs and all prefer situation near the sea—they are especially plentiful on the shores of the Mediterranean. The floral organs for the most part are five in number. Sometimes called the Leadwort Family.

ARMERIA
PLUMBAGO
STATICE

ARMERIA

The Armerias have narrow, grasslike foliage growing in compact clumps; the slender flower stems rise well above it—two characteristics which have given the popular name Sea Pink. The blooms, however, although pinkish in color, are not at all like the Pink in form.

Although good as a border edging, they are especially adapted to rock gardening. Species do not differ greatly: it is usually a matter of color. The best known is A. maritima, pink, and A. maritima var. alba, white. It blooms from May to July. It is to this species that the old-fashioned name, Thrift, rightfully belongs, although all Armerias may be so called without inaccuracy. A. plantaginea is similar; flowers a bit lighter, plant a bit taller. A. formosa is a darker pink; A. alpina, almost purple.

Ordinary soil and increase by division taking care that the parent plants are well watered afterwards; they are a bit sulky when disturbed.

Unaccountable as it may seem, the name is the Latin word for Sweet William!

PLUMBAGO

In common with the family name, Plumbago is from plumbum, lead. It was used for the distressing disease, Lumbago.

P. capensis, of the Forget-me-not blue blooms, is a tropical shrub and may be grown elsewhere only under glass. There is a less known species, P. larpentæ, which is hardy. A dwarf, spreading of habit and in late summer covered by a mass of deep blue flowers.

Rich soil and increase by division as soon as the shoots appear above the ground.

STATICE

Flowers of both annuals and perennials form branching trusses. One of the members of the family with dry blooms. Excellent, when cut, throughout the winter. Blossoms of the annuals, although smallish, are larger than those of the perennials, which are so tiny as to seem a cloudy overtone for any neighbor—like perennial Gypsophila.

The spikes of S. Caspia are 2 to 3 feet high, the flowers, soft lavender. S. latifolia, 2 feet high, is deep blue. The name is from statizo, to stop, because of the astringency of some species.

The roots go deep and do not like to be disturbed. Give good soil mixed with sand, sunny location and *leave alone*. Increase by seed or cuttings.

THE POLEMONIACEÆ

A temperate family, both in nature and habitat. Often called, the Phlox Family, because of its one necessary member. What, I pray you, would midsummer in Gardenland appear were this not there? One shudders to think!

PHLOX

POLEMONIUM

PHLOX

Hardy, named from phlox, a flame, because of brilliant coloring, easy of culture, easier of division, delicately fragrant, August the month of supreme bloom—a perfect plant! Any good soil will satisfy, only be sure to water during dry weather.

P. divariana canadensis blooms in April or May, a heavenly blue, nice with the flowering bulbs of that time, Tulips especially. It grows about a foot high.

P. subulata, Moss or Mountain Phlox is among the first things in the garden to flower. It forms compact masses of moss-like foliage which is good ground covering throughout the season.

Last and best, P. decussata, the hybrids of which are the tall midsummer flowering sorts of the beautiful trusses. Each year finds new varieties. The color range is from white to deep crimson; you may have the characteristic "eye" or not as you choose. According to kind, they begin flowering from early July to August, the catalogues will tell. As soon as withered cut away and a second blooming may follow. The size of trusses depend somewhat on variety; all are bettered by division every third year.

POLEMONIUM

Deeply cut or divided leaves and bell-shaped flowers of blue are characteristic. Although they will succeed without, all species prefer rich soil. They may be divided either in spring or fall or grown from seed.

P. cœruleum, called Jacob's Ladder, is a native of the British Isles. It grows two feet high and blooms in early summer—light blue.

P. reptans is a creeper and yet not one to lose its head and devastate everything within reach. The loosely panicled blooms of deep blue (occasionally white) appear early; the glossy foliage is good throughout the season either in rockery or border. Sometimes called Greek Valerian, this for appearance, it is North American in origin.

The name means war. Why should this be given? For the very good reason—the gospel according to Pliny, that its discovery led to war. There have been less reasonable causes.

THE PRIMULACEÆ

A family of spring: if for no other reason, this would endear them to the gardener. Low of growth and dainty in color, they are better for partial shade. Many are Alpines and most of them prefer cold climate. On the other hand a few, among them the Cyclamens, are tropical.

DODECATHEON (*Shooting Star*)
PRIMULA (*Primrose*)

DODECATHEON

Although this name was given by Pliny to a plant with a lettuce-like leaf, the Dodecatheons of modern time are natives of North America. For this reason they are often called American Cowslips. They are shade-loving and, although they will live in ordinary soil, delight in that enriched by leaf-mold sharpened by a bit of sand. Moisture is a necessity. Increased by seed sown as soon as ripe or division in spring.

D. meadia is the only species listed as hardy. The leaves, although dark in color, are somewhat similar in shape to old-fashioned lettuce and grow in low tufts. From these, in June, rise stalks from eight to ten inches, bearing terminal umbels of bloom. These are light pink, on rare occasion white, and because of their shape merit the popular name, Shooting Star. Excellent for the rockery and good for an edging.

PRIMULA

The genus which gives the family its name, and rightly; there is nothing in it so lovely. P. vulgaris, the world-known English Primrose (she of the "river brink") is said to be the parent of all the polyantha kinds we use in garden and greenhouse. If there is truth in the saying that a child to be as good as his parent must be better, these are inferior. They are large, more varied, useful, even necessary—but not its equal in charm.

They like rich, well-drained soil, which by the way does not mean a dry location; moisture is needful. May be grown from seed with the intriguing possibility of a new color in consequence; also easy to divide after blossom-time or in the fall. You may have varieties of P. vulgaris in widely different shades, reds, lilacs, roses, mauves, violets. This is also true of the polyantha which, in addition, may be bi-colored. They bloom early, as the name from primus, first, would indicate. Charming both in rockery and as edging.

There is a myth of the classic age to the effect that the plant was originally a human being. This time, a man, one Paralisos, son of Flora and Priapus. He died of the malady known as broken heart because of the loss of his sweetheart. And the gods who have understanding for this sort of thing, changed him into the Primrose. It is mere conjecture, yet I hold to the pleasant theory that at some future time, there will be a better English story intertwined with its roots; from some rustic happening mayhaps and certainly cheerful. You probably all know that Disraeli chose it as his emblem and that even now, Primrose Day is observed throughout England.

THE RANUNCULACEÆ

A large family whose type flower is the Buttercup or, botanically speaking, the Ranunculus, which means a little frog. It is also called the Crowfoot Family, because of deeply cleft leaves.

Most of the members are native of the temperate zone. Many are used medicinally and, as it is sometimes a short step from drug to poison, this substance when concentrated in the roots is dangerous. This is especially true with the Aconites and should be remembered if there are children of inquiring mind about.

ACONITUM (*Monkshood*)
ACTÆA (*Baneberry*)
ANEMONE
AQUILEGIA (*Columbine*)
CIMICIFUGA (*Black Snakeroot*)
DELPHINIUM (*Larkspur*)
HELLEBORE NIGER (*Christmas Rose*)
HEPATICA
PÆONIA (*Peony*)
THALICTRUM
TROLLIUS (*Globe Flower*)

ACONITUM

The botanical name, Aconitum, was given because the plant is plentiful near Ancona. The blossoms are borne on tall spikes lifted well above its green leaves. The upper petal is so shaped as to have earned several descriptive names: in England and America it is called Monkshood; in Denmark, Troll's Hat; in Norway, Odin's Helmet; in Germany, Iron Hat—and quite universally, Devil's Herb, because of its poisonous root.

It has always been associated with evil. In myth it is dedicated to Hecate, queen of hell, and was supposed to have been planted there by Cerberus, the three-headed guardian to this unpleasant place. There is also a tale that Medea offered a cup of its juice to Theseus and he, enchanted by her beauty, was about to pledge her health when he chanced to look directly in her eyes and found them glittering and snakelike. Upon her refusal to join in the drink, he dashed the goblet to the floor of marble and this cracked. The marble, mind you, not the goblet, which is a vivid way of saying that Aconite is strong poison.

Why do we grow a thing of such sinister repute in our gardens? Because, for us, the power of Hecate and Medea and hell (?) have passed, and the fact remains that this is a beautiful plant. To be sure, one must never forget that poisonous root, yet it is not the custom to dine on products of the herbaceous border.

It is slow in establishing itself, so do not expect much of it for a year or two and do not disturb a plant till it has grown too large for the space you care to give it. Until such time increase by seed sown when ripe. A. napellus, from 3 to 4 feet high, has dark blue blooms in midsummer; A. autumnale, from 2 to 3 feet, is later and slightly darker in color.

ACTÆA

The blooms of Actæa are small and whitish; they grow in spikes and are not especially interesting. It is for the later fruit, they are given place in a planting. A. alba has berries of pearly white; A. rubra, red: both are decorative for fall effect. They like rich soil and partial shade. About two feet high. Perhaps best suited to the wild garden.

The botanical name is from aktaia, the Elm, on account of the shape of the leaves. They are often called Baneberry.

ANEMONE

Named for the wind, which is fitting; the more sturdy sorts will flourish in exposed places and, like the Daffodil, "Take the winds of March with beauty." When planting for the garden, however, one should remember that the March of the poet was an English one and, further, that even there, this is a reference to the early Anemones of the woods. Although fragile in appearance, these are strong little fellows. They may be transplanted to the rock-garden, yet when one remembers the wealth of material for this purpose, it seems unnecessary to tear them from their native habitat. There is a thrill in finding them in their woodsy home, which is lost elsewhere.

There are varieties more suited to the garden. With one regal exception these are early of bloom. First to come will be A. pulsatilla (the Pasque Flower). It actually does blossom during Eastertide, even in a northern garden. Possibly it is better suited to the rockery than the border. The foliage is deeply cleft, as is the way with this family, and remains good throughout the season. The tulip-shaped blooms of lavender, with their deep yellow stamens for contrast, seem exotic at this time of early flowering. A fascinating blossom from downy budhood to developed fruit.

A. nemorosa is the variety usually known as the Wind Flower: the Germans call it, Little Wind Flower, to distinguish it from larger relatives often given the same popular name.

There is planting direction in nemorosa, which means shade-loving. The bloom is early and the plant from four to eight inches high. Increase by division at any time—spring-flowering Anemones are not exacting in this respect or as to soil condition, yet all prefer moisture and partial shade.

A. canadensis is a taller plant which flowers in June. The blossoms are white and from one-half to an inch across. Easily increased by division; as matter of fact, unless checked, it inclines to spread unpleasantly.

I do not include A. coronaria which, especially in the strain, St. Brigid, is charming. This is for no lack of appreciation: they are the color bearers of the species and, in addition, resemble my great friend, Poppy. But, without special care and protection, they are unsuited to the climatic conditions of our northern gardens.

And now for the aristocrat of them all, A. Japonica. It differs from others in that it must be planted in the spring; also, it flowers in the fall, so late in fact that there are often few blooms save those of the Composites to keep it company. Growing in the border among these, it seems like a bit of misplaced spring. It should be kept moist: as soon as buds have formed, water thoroughly every day. The blooms are borne on loose sprays from three to four feet high according to richness of soil and amount of water. They may be red, mauve or white—single or double as you choose. For beauty in perfection, the single white with its contrast of guinea gold stamens is best. The plant is slow to accustom itself to new ground and, once established, should not be disturbed. Increase by cuttings; it seldom ripens seeds. Good drainage is imperative, else it will winter kill. There is an earlier blooming, more dwarf variety (A. hupehensis), popularly called Chinese Anemone. Like its more stately relative, it likes cool, rich soil yet will withstand drought and the rigors of climate better.

There are many myths for Anemone—always the wee one of the woods. It is said that this is the first flower to answer the soft call of Zephyrus when he tells the world of green things that another spring has come. Small wonder, when one remembers that in classic time, Anemone was a maid beloved of this same god of the West Wind. Alas, the love of such is the love of a day and so this idyll was short of life. Probably the parting was without bitterness; for before Sir Zephyrus blew away for other conquest, he changed the deserted one to the flower which bears her name.

Because of its early flowering, it is associated with Easter, and in many parts of Europe is still known as the Easter or Resurrection Flower.

Venus, too, has a certain claim; this from another and quite different tale of its origin. When Adonis lay dying, the grieving love-goddess bent over him and some of her tears fell to the ground. These, of course, were too precious to be lost and the earth changed them to Anemones.

AQUILEGIA

The word Aquilegia is derived from aquila, the eagle, given because the sepals and petals of the bloom taken together look like a bird in flight. It is for the same reason that the better known popular name Columbine, from columba, the dove, seems fitting.

A. canadensis is the wild Columbine of the woods; that dainty bit of red and yellow which nods to the tune of the winds of early spring. It is successful in the rock-garden, the fern-like foliage good for the season. One caution—do not plant near cultivated varieties; all Aquilegias cross readily and the result of this combination is not usually successful. One earnest request—buy seeds or plants. It is not difficult to transplant from the woods but in name of all that is gentle and of good repute, leave these wildlings for the enjoyment of those who go a'Maying!

A. cœrulea, called Rocky Mountain Columbine, is one of our most beautiful native plants. The sepals of the flower are dark blue and the petals white. It is taller, blooms later and longer, and is not so widely distributed as A. canadensis.

Columbine is a plant which is loveliest in the long-spurred, hybrid forms, especially those of the Mrs. Scott Elliott strain; the blooms are large and the spurs, as the name suggests, unusually long. There is a wide choice of color, mauve, lavender, purple, blue, cream, yellow, pink, red; either contrasted or combined with white. The time of heavy bloom is early summer: this may be lengthened fully a month by allowing no seeds to form. The foliage is good throughout the season and is excellent massed or placed singly as soft relief next to some plant of coarse leaf.

It is an alluring adventure to allow a few seedpods to ripen; there is always the possibility of a new color combination as result. If, on the other hand, you want to be sure of increasing any favorite, make a root division—this is the only sure method. Aquilegias will grow in almost any soil yet respond to enrichment.

CIMICIFUGA

A native plant which is good for a moist, shady part of the border, although it will grow almost anywhere. C. racemosa, the only variety worthy place in the border, grows from four to six feet high and gives rather the appearance of a shrub. The leaves, although deeply cleft like more delicate growth of this family, are large and inclined to coarseness. The white, feathery blooms come in August and are borne on drooping racemes. There is nothing especially distinguished about either foliage or flower but the plant will do yeoman's service as a filler. Ordinary soil, even a bit on the poor side suffices. Increase by division.

The name is from cimex, a bug, and fugo, to drive away, because it is reputed to be distasteful to insects. It is a fact that, for cross-fertilization, the flower must depend on the fly rather than the bee. Popularly called Black Snakeroot, Black Cohosh, or Bugbane.

DELPHINIUM

Better known as Larkspur, a name given because the long sepal looks like a spur. The word, Delphinium, is from delphin, a dolphin—the flower was considered enough like a dolphin's head to merit this.

Blue is the color of this queen of the June garden. This may be either of the lightest or darkest, with intermediate shades. Lavender too, has been introduced by the hybridizers and there have been attempts at white—not as yet altogether successful.

It will grow acceptably in any good garden soil, but responds generously to special treatment, giving taller spikes of bloom and finer foliage. If you wish the best possible Delphiniums, buy roots of such fine strains as the Vanderbilt hybrids. Have the soil prepared by deep digging and the addition of well-rotted manure. Plant in the fall. The following spring, as soon as growth begins, dig in a little bone-meal. Give plenty of water during growth and up to the time of bloom. As soon as this first flowering has passed, cut the entire plant to the ground, enrich again, and you will have a second blooming.

The plant is at its best during the second and third years of bloom. On this account, it is well to keep a supply of seedlings to take the place of plants which have passed this period.

The arch-enemy is a leaf disease called, Black Spot.

To keep this in check, spray both ground and foliage with bordeaux mixture *before it appears.* If any plant is affected dig it up and burn. Give a dressing of lime in the fall and, after frost a light covering of coal ashes—this last for the discouragement of slugs.

HELLEBORE

Hellebore is derived from helein, to kill, and bora, food—the roots of many varieties are poisonous. There are several species suited to a warm climate; only one (H. niger) will be permanent elsewhere. This seems a bit contradictory when one remembers that they all bloom out of doors during the winter months. The blossoming time for H. niger in England begins in December, but in a climate such as that of New England, this is retarded till February. It is a native of Central Europe and West Asia and flowers there throughout the winter.

The leaves are leathery in texture; the flowers, which are like a single wild rose in form, are white, occasionally tinged pink. Probably blossoming at any other time, the plant would seem of little garden value: when one remembers that it is possible to dig through snow and find bloom, it becomes precious. It is usually called Christmas Rose and is in great demand in the flower-markets of the Old World at Yuletide.

A difficult plant to increase. This must be done either by root-cutting taken just after bloom period, with the chance of losing a plant, or by the slow method of seed germination. Seeds should be sown as soon as ripe in gritty soil and kept cool. The plant requires rich, loamy soil, moisture and shade.

From early times, the Hellebores were considered cure for various ills ranging from slight indisposition to insanity. The story of the origin of Christmas Rose is more pleasing. On the night of the Nativity, when the shepherds were "sore afraid," a few of the more daring followed the Magi and were rewarded by a sight of the Christ Child. Now it happened that the young sister of one of them went along too. She saw the rich gifts laid at His feet and turned away, grieving that she had nothing to offer. As she was returning to her home in the hills, an angel met her and asked why she was sad. After this messenger from heaven had learned the reason, he touched the ground with a lily he was carrying and, lo, it was covered with blossoms. The child gathered an armful and quickly ran back to the Manger and the Infant, disregardful of the gold and precious stones, stretched out His tiny hands for the flowers.

HEPATICA

The earliest flower of spring. As soon as snow has melted and regardless of weather condition, the wee blooms of white, flushed with pink or blue, appear. There seems a bit of white magic in this daring, because they are without leaves to bear company.

The nurseryman's catalogue will usually tell you that flowers come before the leaves, which is well enough as a garden statement but not true as scientific fact. It is a law of nature that a plant must first produce leaf, then flower. How do we square this with the apparently contradictory habit of a certain few—Hepatica for one? We must observe what may be called the season's cycle of an individual plant. In case of Hepatica, it is this. Seed germinates and develops leaves which live throughout one summer and a good part of the following winter. These, then, wither and disappear. The following spring—flowers appear. Because this plant is perennial, it will repeat all other cycles from root instead of seed. So you see, in this case as all others, *leaf comes before flower.*

Hepatica is charming as a rock-garden subject, not alone because of early bloom; the heart-shaped leaves are unusual. It prefers rich soil, moisture and partial shade. Increase by division in the fall.

The name comes from hepaticos, which means related to the liver, and was given because of the shape of the leaves. It is sometimes called Liverleaf, a custom which I, for one, deplore.

PÆONIA

Peony, that gorgeous creation which is said to be the only flower sufficiently a rival to make the Rose jealous, is too widely known to need description. For many years, it has been a favorite and may be found in stately planting and farmhouse yard alike. It always has prominent place in the summer flower shows and, of late years, has merited the dignity of shows of its own.

We love it for its virtues—ornamental foliage which is especially beautiful before blossom time; delicate fragrance; blooms that may be enormous and at the same time, never coarse. When grown under proper condition (partial shade and enrichment) it is not subject to disease and unusually free from insect pests. Perhaps its only limitation is shortness of flowering season, and even this may be a wise provision lest our gardens run over-much to Peonies.

There are many double and an increasing number of single named varieties. Do not chance unnamed kinds: Peony is too regal a lady to treat with discourtesy. Price ranges from fifty cents to a hundred dollars and let me stress that the less costly are not of necessity the less lovely. The reason for such difference is in the amount of stock available. It is a long, expensive task to make a new variety. Seed is slow to germinate and a plant does not come into bloom for at least three years.

Even then, although parentage is good and it give every indication of aristocratic worth, the flower may prove worthless.

For best result, enrich the soil two feet deep and set three feet apart, keeping the crown above ground. Before bloom period, dress with a good fertilizer and water abundantly. Cultivate carefully lest the roots be injured and, sad necessity, disbud. In the fall, cut away all foliage that winter winds may not disturb the roots. It is the old tradition not to divide roots until blooms begin to deteriorate. Although the plant does not take kindly to disturbance, this is a mistake: the time to divide is *before* deterioration. After a plant has reached full growth, every third year is none too often. Division should be made in the early fall.

There are several stories of the name's origin. One states that Apollo took it in his capacity as healer when he was caring for the wounds of the gods at the time of the Trojan war. Another tells of how a mortal, called Pæon, cured an injury for Pluto and, by so doing, roused the ire of Æsculapius who put him to death, and that Pluto changed him to a flower. Still another says that it was not a physician at all but Pæonia, a shepherdess, loved by Apollo, for whom the plant is named. There is a charming myth to the effect that the flower sprang from a moonbeam—not difficult to understand if one sees a white bloom under the touch of night's Enchantress.

THALICTRUM

A plant which is especially valuable because of its foliage which, in all species, is deeply cleft and a light touch to either garden or bouquet. The name, from thallo, to grow green, was given because the young shoots are unusually light in color. All may be divided either in the spring or early fall and are satisfied with ordinary soil. The flowers, which grow in decorative clusters, are unusual in that the stamens are their most prominent and attractive feature.

T. adiantifolium has foliage as delicate as that of Maidenhair Fern. The blooms are whitish green and come in June.

T. aquilegifolium, as the name implies, has leaves like Columbine. The flowers are purple and appear in June or July. From two to three feet high.

T. dioicum, called Early Meadow Rue, is shorter (from one to one and a half feet) and blossoms earlier. The flowers may be either purple or green. The plant has the merit of succeeding in shade.

T. polygamum, Tall Meadow Rue, becomes a stately plant when given rich, moist soil. The flowers are white and unusual in those of garden worth, apetalous. The word, polygamum, in botany, means that there are staminate, pistillate and perfect flowers. In case of T. polygamum, these may grow either on the same or different plants.

TROLLIUS

Trollius, from a German word meaning, globe, is often called Globe Buttercup, which is an accurate description for foliage, bud and blossom; the difference is in size. T. europæus has slightly fragrant flowers of pale yellow: T. caucasicus is orange and, alas, without scent. Both grow about two feet high and blossom from June to August.

They will succeed in ordinary soil but are improved by enrichment and moisture. Increase by root division, preferably in autumn. To raise from seed is a slow process; under the most favorable conditions it will be three years before one may hope for a sizable plant.

THE ROSACEÆ

An immensely useful family in horticulture and, when one remembers that without it there could be no rose-gardens, for the Queen of Flowers is of its members, it must be admitted that no word of commendation is necessary. Rather, a humble gratitude.

Apple, crab, pear, quince, plum, cherry, peach, apricot, too, walk under its banner to the delight of beauty- and fruit-loving man. And all the Hawthornes, which might be used more than they are in floriculture.

GEUM (*Avens*)
POTENTILLA
SPIRÆA

GEUM

A word of explanation before we consider this plant. Just as the Lily was banished from the Liliaceæ because it is a bulb, so must the Rose be omitted from the Rosaceæ because it is a shrub. To be sure, it is not generally considered so and I would most willingly break a rule for its sweet sake were it not that the literature devoted to it is legion and written by experts whose knowledge of its various types and needs is far greater than mine.

And now, for the Geum. The name, from geyo, to stimulate, was given because the roots of some species have medicinal quality similar to that of Peruvian bark and quinine. Small plants with large, rose-like flowers. They may be increased by seed or division in the spring. Give a sandy loam enriched by leaf-mold, sunny situation and an abundance of water.

Scarlet is the characteristic color, although G. heldreichi is dark orange and Lady Stratcheden, yellow. Perhaps G. Lady Bradshaw is the best, a brilliant scarlet and particularly effective at the front of the border.

POTENTILLA

How many plants have been supposed to possess medicinal quality! Some, to be sure, have been proven otherwise in a more scientific age. Yet, as in this case, the fact lingers in a name. Potens means powerful, as a student of even first year Latin will know.

It is often called, Cinquefoil, because there are five petals; the bloom is like that of the Strawberry in form. Increase by seed or division in spring.

P. repustris has white flowers borne on long stems and will thrive under dry condition. There are other varieties, both double and single, all, less known.

SPIRÆA

Spiræa, which means a wreath in reference to the blossom-form of several species, is much more often a shrub than herbaceous. An interesting characteristic of the genus is the great number of stamens, sometimes as many as sixty, which prove an ornamental feature of the blossoms. They succeed in ordinary soil and grow to luxury with enrichment. Give them half shade and moisture. Seeds may be sown when ripe or in the autumn; otherwise division must be made by root-cuttings.

The foliage is fern-like and the blooms borne on tall, many-branching spikes. There are various hybrids with colored flowers, although to my mind, the white of S. filipendula is best. Named varieties are worth the slight difference in price, because the life of a plant is long.

THE RUTACEÆ

That this family is more abundant in South Africa and Australia and least in North Africa is indication that it chooses warm, yet not tropical growing condition. Sometimes known as the Rue Family from members congenial to the temperate zone. Including Prickly Pear, Orange and Lemon trees—is it too much to say that genera differ widely in climatic adaptability? One characteristic is common to them all; glossy dark green leaves, which are often compound.

DICTAMNUS (*Fraxinella*)
RUTA

DICTAMNUS

The plant, growing about two feet high, is bushy in form. The compound, glossy green leaves are good throughout the season and excellent contrast for neighbors of lighter shade or as background for flowers.

The season of bloom is short and in June. D. ruber has a pinkish-red flower which grows in clusters. It has been given the name Gas Plant because of an unpleasant odor: also Burning Bush, not for color but the curious fact that it throws off a gas which *occasionally* will ignite. A variety, alba is far better; the flowers are white and the gaseous exhalation less marked.

Both prefer light, well drained soil and full sun. They are not easy to increase. Seed germinates slowly and under the most favorable condition, it will be three years before a plant from it is large enough for the border. Another method, that of root-cutting, has the disadvantage of the sacrifice of a plant. Fortunately, they live many years and improve with age.

The name was given by Vergil: it has a second, Fraxinella, the diminutive of the Latin word for Ash—this because of the resemblance of the leaves to those of the tree.

RUTA

Rutas, from rus, to flow, because of a medicinal quality of some herb species; as matter of candor, are for the most part strong smelling herbs used in cooking or medicinally. There is one species, R. patavina, which is good for the rockery. It has fine-cut leaves and light yellow blossoms which grow in compact heads.

Sandy soil with lime; increase by seed or cuttings in autumn. Once established, it will take care of itself, a desirable quality in the rock-garden. Often called, Padua Rue.

THE SAXIFRAGACEÆ

A large family, which prefers cold climate as the tiny wildling of the woods called, Saxifrage, would suggest. There are many herb and shrub members: among the shrubs, such aids to good living as Currant and Gooseberry and to good plantings as Hydrangea, Deutzia and Philadelphus.

ASTIBLE
HEUCHERA (*Coral Bells*)
MITELLA
TIARELLA (*Foam Flower*)

ASTIBLE

To begin, let me correct a misapprehension about the family connections of the Astibles. Because of their similar form of growth, they are often confused with the Spireas. A few nurserymen go even so far as to list them as Spireas with Astible as a secondary name, while practically all others who offer the seeds or plants for sale, do so under the name "Astible, Herbaceous Spirea." As matter of fact, these two are in no way related: Spirea is a genus of Family Rosaceæ while Astible, as classified here, is of the Saxifragaceæ. The name, from a, not, and stilbe, bright—given because the individual flowerets are small—is from the Greek.

These flowerets are massed in loose panicles so striking in appearance as to make the name's derivation seem inappropriate. They flower in midsummer and are at their best with rich soil, partial shade and an abundance of water. Increase by division.

It is the better plan to buy plants of named varieties. The cost is higher than of those less distinguished, but the roots live long and may be divided after their first season with you. Make your own choice from a reliable seedsman's catalogue.

HEUCHERA

Heuchera, named for Heuher, a German botanist, is charming either as an edging or in the rock-garden. The heart-shaped leaves grow low and remain good throughout the season. From June to July, dainty clusters of bell-like bloom, borne on stiff, slender stems, rise well about the foliage. The plant has been called Coralbell, Crimsonbell, or the contradictory, White Coralbell, according to varietal color.

Increase by division, either in spring or fall. Ordinary garden soil is sufficient; good drainage imperative. You may have scarlet, white or coral—the coral best because its shade is unusual in blossom life. Excellent for cutting and especially well adapted for flower arrangements.

MITELLA

A low-growing plant suited to the rockery. The tiny blooms are white and borne on racemes from six to eight inches high. May and June are the flowering months. M. diphylla is the best variety. The leaves grow in tufts and are good till frost.

Give partial shade and ordinary garden soil. Increase by division in the fall.

The name origin is interesting. It is the diminutive of mitra, miter—a little miter, because the seedpods resemble this symbol of ecclesiastical dignity. For the same reason, it is often popularly known as Bishop's Cap.

TIARELLA

An obliging plant: hardy; easily increased by division; at home in sandy soil; will grow in partial shade or full sunshine—its one necessity is plenty of water.

The foliage of T. cordifolia (the best) is light green in the spring and changes with the waning season to a reddish bronze. The creamy, star-shaped flowers are massed on a stem lifted above the leaves: they are so dainty as to be popularly called, Foam Flowers. An early bloomer.

The botanical name is diminutive for tiara. As is the case with Mitella, this was given because of the shape of the seedpods.

THE SCROPHULARIACEÆ

No name in Flowerland comes so haltingly from my pen. It speaks for itself, alas—a certain variety was used as remedy for an unpleasant disease. What travesty that the beauty of other members should be condemned to bear it!

The family is widely distributed and, as is usual in such case, not exacting as to growing conditions. The juices are often acrid: some of these, Digitalis for one, are used medicinally.

CHELONE (*Turtlehead*)
DIGITALIS (*Foxglove*)
PENTSTEMON
VERBASCUM (*Mullein*)
VERONICA

CHELONE

Chelone means tortoise and was given to this plant because of the shape of the flower—the upper part of the two-lipped corolla suggests the back of a tortoise. It is also called Turtlehead; in form, the bloom is a vegetable reproduction of the head of this creature of long life. Blossoms are clustered at the end of strong stems.

It grows from two to three feet high with lance-like leaves of dark green. Especially effective near a brook or pond. Give rich soil mixed with a bit of sand. Increase by division.

C. Lyoni has purple flowers; C. glabra, white, tipped with deep pink. Both are late in blossoming.

DIGITALIS

Better known as Foxglove. It is biennial for the most part yet requires little extra care on this account because it self-seeds freely. Just be sure not to mistake the wee plants for weeds and you may reasonably expect a continuous garden supply. It is well to take a few when ripe for the cold-frame too. In all species it is a stately thing with tall spikes of bloom. Although it will grow in ordinary soil, enrichment adds height to the blooming stalks.

D. ambigua is a perennial with yellow flowers and flowering stalks somewhat shorter than those of the biennials. The biennial, D. gloxiniæflora is the best; when richly fed, it will reach a height of from four to five feet. Blooms may be white, pink, rose, purple and dotted with crimson or brown. From June to July is the blossom time.

It is sometimes called Fairy Thimble, especially in rural England. Both popular and botanical names were given because of the shape of the individual flower—Digitalis means a finger stall or covering.

PENTSTEMON

Pentstemon means, literally, five stamens; examine a blossom and you will find one abortive and four fertile stamens. Although P. pubescens, native to our woods, is a charming wildling, the hybrider has taken P. Hartwegi, from Mexico, and made forms vastly better for the garden.

These at first, although perennial, proved tender and were usually treated as annuals. Now, they have been taught to forget the heat of their native birthplace. A bit of extra cover during winter months still pleases them and good drainage is a necessity. Give ordinary soil and increase by cuttings of the non-flowering stalks or by seed. This is one of the herbaceous plants which blooms soon from the time of seed-sowing.

The following have been found hardy: P. barbatus Torreyi, scarlet; P. barbatus, Pink Beauty; P. ovatus, blue or purple—all flower in midsummer. There are other species worth a trial as to weather condition and sure of welcome from standpoint of color. The Pentstemons have a future—if I may be allowed the dangerous privilege of prophecy.

VERBASCUM

Call it Verbascum, from barbascum, bearded, and like as not the gardener will consider it a useful and decorative plant. Call it Mullein—and it may be banished as a weed. Which only goes to show that gardeners, in common with other folk, are not always wise.

The silvery gray leaves are cool delight; it will grow in any soil, withstand drought, bloom in midsummer. V. thapsus is the species of field and roadside. Nurserymen also offer hybrid forms which are sometimes taller and may have flowers of white, rose or purple as well as yellow.

VERONICA

There was a time when the mention of Veronica brought to mind a plant with green lance-like leaves and spikes of blue bloom about two feet in height. This of course, because only one species was generally known.

Now, this is all changed: Veronica may be white or shades of blue, pink or lavender; the foliage may range from dark green to a gray so light as to seem almost white. Also, you may have blooms much higher than two feet or wee growth for the rockery three or four inches high. A useful, versatile and, above all, beautiful plant whose only limitation is the lack of fragrance. Tall sorts usually flower during midsummer; if not allowed to seed, there will be a second blooming. The dwarfs, as a whole, blossom earlier.

I do not mention varieties—there are too many. Just consult the nurseryman's catalogue and, if your gardening condition requires this, have a care that you choose those listed as hardy. Give ordinary soil and full sunshine. Increase by division in the spring. The dwarfs often develop roots at the points of the stem and these may be cut for new plants at any time.

Sometimes called Speedwell, unfortunately to my mind, when botany has dedicated it to St. Veronica.

THE SOLANACEÆ

A family which may be distinguished by alternate leaves. It has a preference for warm climate and yet such annuals as Nicotiana, Petunia, Salpiglossis, Schizanthus are to be found in northern gardens; potato, tomato and eggplant, too, grow wherever there is kitchen-gardening. Tobacco, the cayenne pepper plant and various tonic-and narcotic-giving trees and herbs flourish only in tropical heat.

The blooms of all the family are attractive and sometimes fragrant. Many open after sundown, which explains the popular name, Nightshade Family.

PHYSALIS (*Chinese Lantern Plant*)

PHYSALIS

Physalis Francheti, although a native of Japan, is called Chinese Lantern Plant. The blossoms are whitish and inconspicuous. Never cut them because it is for the sake of the fruit that the plant is grown. When the petals have withered, the calyx forms a wee ball of green which by magic all its own begins to swell—the name from phusa, a bladder, describes this quality. When fully grown it is two or three inches in radius and in fall turns to orange-scarlet. Several hang on one stem and if the leaves are stripped away, make colorful winter decoration indoors. The tender plant popularly known as Winter Cherry because of its gay fruit to be seen at the florist's during the winter months, is also a Physalis (P. Alkekengi).

P. Francheti is hardy and in rich, well-drained soil, about two feet high. May be raised from seed, although by doing so one must sacrifice the "lantern"; cuttings after bloom or by root division. If the latter is the method you choose, wait till leaves and stalks have died away.

THE UMBELLIFERÆ

Blooms take the umbel or umbrella form; one thinks of Queen Anne's Lace, lovely weed of the field, as shelter for a fairy. Dainty of flower and sturdy of growth, as hemlock, parsnip, carrot, and parsley attest. As further proof, this is sometimes called the Parsley Family.

It likes cool condition; in fact when found in the tropics, this is always in the mountains.

ERYNGIUM (*Sea Holly*)

ERYNGIUM

The name is an adaptation from the original, erygeon, given by Pliny. Called Sea Holly, because of the glossy foliage. The plant has distaste for wet feet and a wish for full sun. For better and stronger increase, take seed.

E. amethystinum has thistle-like heads of lavender. It grows 2 to 3 feet and is somewhat straggly.

E. alpinus, 1 to 2 feet, is a rich though metallic blue.

Two species, E. campestre and martimum, are aromatic and when dried and sugared known as Eringo-root.

THE VALERIANACEÆ

A small family found in the northern part of the Old World. Delicate foliage and fragrance which is exotic for such situation make it welcome. Some species have tonic value; in fact the name was given for this reason; Valerius used it as medicine.

VALERIANA (*Hardy Heliotrope*)

VALERIANA

Valeriana officinalis is popularly called Hardy Heliotrope because of its heliotrope-like fragrance. Otherwise it does not resemble the plant of this name; the blue-green leaves are fine-cut and grow in low, dense masses. Above these in June and July, tall flowering-stalks are lifted. Individual bloom is infinitesimal and clustered in soft heads. The color is pinkish white; it is the haunting fragrance which makes it a garden necessity. Not alone to the human race as Cat Valerian, another popular name would indicate. The tiger-of-the-house likes it sometimes too well and rolls in it to its damage: rats and mice too have a feeling for it expressed in gnawing of the roots.

Ordinary soil. It spreads rapidly and self-sows too. As the life of an individual plant is long, once it is admitted to the garden, you may be assured that it will remain there.

Species V. jatamansi is used for perfume and has been from times of long ago. It was necessary part of all precious ointments of the East—there is legend that it was in that poured upon the feet of the Savior by the Magdalen. Today, wherever incense rises, it is there.

A tale from the Hindu is to the effect that emergency separated a man from his wife the day of the marriage. Before he went away, he led her to his garden and, showing her a plant of Valerian said, "I will be safe so long as this flourishes." Years passed and when at last the weary traveler returned, in true oriental legend style, he came in the rags of a beggar. To his happiness, on entering his garden, he found that his Valerian had grown to tree-like proportion and that his wife stood trimming the branches.

"And they lived happily ever after."

THE VIOLACEÆ

It may come as surprise to many that this family is largely tropical and usually of the shrub-form; also that the roots of a few have emetic quality. One genus, Viola, will also shed sweetness in the temperate zone and gives both nature and the perfumer the fragrance of Violet.

VIOLA

VIOLA

To begin, let me say that there is a certain confusion between the words, Viola, Violet and Pansy. Shall I add to this when I say that they are all Violas? It is simple considered botanically, just the distinction between the genus and its species. Viola is the genus. Violet and Pansy species, while other species are called Violas and the specific name dropped—this all in unscientific language of course; another case where it is confusing. Species have been crossed and re-crossed till they differ widely both in size and color.

This is especially true of Pansy (V. tricolor). It has been hybridized into many colors and color combinations. When properly grown, in rich soil and partial shade and given constant waterings, the blooms are from an inch to an inch and a half across. If one wishes strong stems and flowers of first quality, these should be picked daily. Sometimes, even when this is the case, they incline to grow straggly in the heat of midsummer. When this is the case, cut back to the roots and strong, new shoots will appear.

The story of the origin of the name is pathetic. Once upon a time a field of Violets was so fragrant as to attract many visitors who, in picking, trampled and bruised the plants. The unfortunate sufferers prayed that their scent be taken away, and it was—even to this day. The name is a corruption of the word pensée, thought. May their wee faces which look up so trustingly from the greenery, give pause to those who would ruthlessly pick blossoms of whatever kind—especially those of field and woods.

Probably everyone knows that the double Violets of the florist are grown under glass. But to see the flower at its best, one must go to the woodland or river bank. They won't be so fat here and for this reason more charming. To say nothing of the perfection of environment. With the exception of one species, Viola odorata (Sweet Violet) they are, alas, without fragrance. This species, which grows wild in the greater part of Europe as well as Northern Africa and Western Asia, is the parent of our sweet scented cultivated Violets, be they white, blue or purple. In the open border they need careful treatment. Rich soil, partial shade, a bit of extra fertilizing (well-rotted manure) when bloom has passed, an occasional watering after sundown.

Classic Greece gives the Violet an interesting origin. Do you recall that when the flirtatious Jupiter was found with Io, a priestess of his wife's temple, he changed the hapless lady to a white heifer? Now a priestess, even thus disguised, cannot relish grass, and so the Violet was made as more suitable fare. Poor Io! Although this blossom was created for her sustenance, it was held to be sacred to Venus. Further, although hitherto considered soothing, once identified with this triumphant lady, it acquired the quality of a stimulant to love. The old gods with their unholy intrigues have passed but the Violet lives and has been dedicated to the Virgin. It sometimes finds place with Lily and Rose on her altar.

There are other tales about it and many verses. I may not tell of them to the neglect of the Violas. These are not grown so generally in this country as in England. Is this because they are not so large as Pansy and without the fragrance of Violet? Happily they are becoming better known. Although like the Violet in form, they have a slender aristocracy all their own. It is wise to treat them as biennials, in fact this applies to all the genus. Grow under the same garden conditions as Pansy and choose the colors you desire from named varieties.

FAMILIES OF FLOWERLAND WE HAVE CONSIDERED

Acanthaceæ (ak-an-thā′sē-ē)
Apocynaceæ (a-pos-i-nā′sē-ē)
Aristolochiaceæ (ar″is-tō-lō-ki-ā′sē-ē)
Asclepiadeæ (as-klē-pī′a-dē)
Bignoniaceæ (big-nō-ni-ā′sē-ē)
Boraginaceæ (bō-raj-i-nā′sē-ē)
Campanulaceæ (kam-pan-ū-lā′sē-ē)
Caryophyllaceæ (kar″-i-ō-fi-lā′sē-ē)
Cistaceæ (sis-tā′-sē-ē)
Commelinaceæ (ko-mel-i-nā′sē-ē)
Compositæ (kom-poz′i-tē)
Crassulaceæ (kras-ū-lā′sē-ē)
Cruciferæ (krö-sif′e-rē)
Dipsacaceæ (dip-sa-kā′sē-ē)
Euphorbiaceæ (ū-fôr-bi-ā′sē-ē)
Gentianaceæ (jen-shia̤-nā′sē-ē)
Hypericeæ (hi-pe̤r-is′ē-ē)
Iridaceæ (ir-i-dā′sē-ē)
Labiatæ (lā-bi-ā′tē)
Leguminocæ (lē-gū-mi-nō′sē)
Liliaceæ (lil-i-ā′sē-ē)
Linaceæ (li-nā′sē-ē)
Malvaceæ (mal-vā′sē-ē)
Onagraceæ (on-a-grā′sē-ē)
Papaveraceæ (pā-pav-e-rā′sē-ē)
Plumbagineæ (plum-ba̤-jin′ē-ē)

Polemoniaceæ (pol-e-mō-ni-ā′sē-ē)
Primulaceæ (prim-ū-lā′sē-ē)
Ranunculaceæ (rā-nung-kū-lā′sē-ē)
Rosaceæ (rō-zā′sē-ē)
Rutaceæ (rò-tā′sē-ē)
Saxifragaceæ (sak″si-frā-gạ̈′sē-ē)
Scrophulariaceæ (skrof-ū-lā-ri-ā′sē-ē)
Solanaceæ (sol-ā-nā′sē-ē)
Umbelliferæ (um-be-lif′e-rē)
Valerianaceæ (vạ̈-lē″-ri-ạ̈-nā′sē-ē)
Violaceæ (vi-ō-lā′sē-ē)

INDEX

INDEX

INDEX